Prekarisierung und soziale Entkopplung – transdisziplinäre Studien

Reihe herausgegeben von

Rolf-Dieter Hepp, Institut für Soziologie, FU Berlin, Berlin, Germany

Robert Riesinger, Journalismus und Public Relations (PR), FH Joanneum Gesellschaft mbH, Graz, Austria

David Kergel, Internationale Hochschule, Duisburg, Germany

Birte Heidkamp-Kergel, E-Learning Zentrum, Hochschule Rhein-Waal, Kamp-Lintfort, Germany

Die Zunahme sozialer Unsicherheit und kultureller Verunsicherung in postfordistischen Gesellschaften erzeugt einen Status Quo, in dem Prozesse der Prekarisierung und der „sozialen Entkopplung" (Robert Castel) verstärkt das Zentrum der Gesellschaft durchziehen. Der Verlust sozialer Garantien führt dabei zur Aushöhlung sozialstaatlicher Errungenschaften. Dadurch werden die Lebenskontexte und das Alltagsleben der Menschen stark verändert.
Das sozialwissenschaftliche Netzwerk S.U.P.I. beschäftigt sich auf europäischer Ebene seit Jahren mit den gegenwärtigen Formen von sozialer Unsicherheit, Prekarität und Ungleichheit. Die Reihe, herausgegeben von Mitgliedern des Netzwerks, präsentiert transdisziplinäre Forschungen zu den sozialen und kulturellen Transformationen in den sozialstaatlich geprägten Demokratien. Sie versteht sich als Forum für die Diskussion in nationalen, europäischen und auch globalen Kontexten. Ebenen einer kritischen Analyse aus multidisziplinären und feldorientierten Perspektiven werden dabei initiiert, aufgenommen und unterstützt. Überschreitung und Öffnung dienen programmatisch als Wegmarken für theoretisch-analytische Beiträge und empirisch-angewandte Forschung.

The increase of social insecurity in post-Fordist societies effect fundamental societal changes. As a consequence Precarity and Disaffiliation (Robert Castel) affecting increasingly the center of society. The loss of social guarantees leads to an erosion of the welfare state. As a result, living situations and everyday life are deeply changed.
The S.U.P.I.-Project (Social Uncertainty, Precarity, Inequality) is an European Research Group established by European and international scholars and experts. The network has been concerned with present forms of social insecurity, precariousness and inequality at European level for years. Edited by members of the network, the book series presents transdisciplinary research on aspects of social and cultural transformations in the democracies which are characterized by the welfare state. The book series opens a discursive space for discussions in national, European and global contexts. The contributions of the book series provide critical analyses from multidisciplinaryperspectives, theoretical-analytical reflections and empirical-applied research.

Rolf Dieter Hepp
Editor

Shifts and Reorientation within the Social-Crisis and Catastrophe: towards the Realization of Pandemic Epistemological Processes

Springer VS

Editor
Rolf Dieter Hepp
Institut für Soziologie
Freie Universität Berlin
Berlin, Germany

ISSN 2509-3266 ISSN 2509-3274 (electronic)
Prekarisierung und soziale Entkopplung – transdisziplinäre Studien
ISBN 978-3-658-43040-5 ISBN 978-3-658-43041-2 (eBook)
https://doi.org/10.1007/978-3-658-43041-2

This Springer VS imprint is published by the registered company Springer Fachmedien Wiesbaden GmbH, part of Springer Nature.
The registered company address is: Abraham-Lincoln-Str. 46, 65189 Wiesbaden, Germany

Paper in this product is recyclable.

Contents

Contributors

Ronald C. Arnett Duquesne University Pittsburgh, Pittsburgh, PA, USA

Vyacheslav Bobkov Institute of Economics, Russian Academy of Sciences, Moscow, Russia

António M. Duarte Faculty of Psychology, University of Lisbon, Lisbon, Portugal

Rolf Dieter Hepp Freie Universität, Berlin, Germany

Peter Herrmann Law School at the Central South University, Changsha, China

Fernando Marhuenda-Fluixá University of Valencia, Valencia, Spain

Lennart Noerrcklit University of Aalborg, Aalborg, Denmark

Elena Odintsova Institute of Economics, Russian Academy of Sciences, Moscow, Russia

Marco Ricceri The Secretary General, EURISPES Institute, Rome, Italy

Igor Shichkin Plekhanov Russian University of Economics, Moscow, Russia

Alexander Sieg Berlin, Germany

As an Introduction. The Revenge of the Nature as Catastrophes

Rolf Dieter Hepp

With Corona, multiple shifts are taking place within society. Here, I would like to refer to virology, which is taking on a different status as a result of the pandemic and entering the center of society. Although virology cannot be characterized as an "orchid science" until 2020, interest in it can only be estimated as relatively low until the 2020 pandemic. The Bertelsmann Foundation still brought out a hospital report in December 2018, according to which, similar to Italy, there were calls for hospitals to be downsized and intensive care units to be closed because they were underutilized. That the number of ICU beds was too high due to lack of utilization and therefore dysfunctional, contributing to losses, or profit cuts.

The 2018 flu epidemic had claimed 25,000 victims in Germany without this penetrating the public consciousness, the Corona epidemic has claimed 83,325 lives in just over a year (by 28.4.2021)

In 2021, the German candidate for chancellor, Laschet, complained that the research results of virologists always contain different interpretations due to new findings, so that as a politician he would have to re-evaluate decisions again and again and would not have a clear, universally valid basis for decision-making. This is a fact that can be applied to any sudden natural disaster or pandemic. At the same time, successful control of nature is called into question here, so that

R. D. Hepp (✉)
Freie Universität, Berlin, Germany
e-mail: falsekerghepp@gmx.de

R. D. Hepp (ed.), *Shifts and Reorientation Within the Social-Crisis and Catastrophe: Towards the Realization of Pandemic Epistemological Processes*, Prekarisierung und soziale Entkopplung – transdisziplinäre Studien,
https://doi.org/10.1007/978-3-658-43041-2_1

this hides, as it were, a grievance of society, since it reveals the inability of an immediate solution to the crisis.

"To the game (of natural science and philosophy, d.A.) a third figure is added - namely the public. Civil society does not understand anything about science and ethical problems, because between philosophy and natural science stand the media. They deal with the problems without having any knowledge of the humanities or the natural sciences. This makes the game extremely convoluted. A dramatic situation could develop from this. So the game consists of four characters who do not understand each other (…). The way out can only be that the scientific, the good information is in the possession of the philosophers, the natural scientists, the media and the public and that everyone is able to construct an ethics on the basis of his knowledge which is at the same time the ethics of all. That would be the ideal situation.

However, we are far from this situation because there is no dialogue between the four figures. To make matters worse, a fifth person is added to the game - the politician." (Serres, 2016)

What natural disasters and pandemics have in common is that they are sketched as an "outside" thing that affects society. However, in this opposition, this does not correspond to social facticity, since both the plague, as well as cholera, as well as Covid 19 were caused from the outside by a specific social action. Plague was spread throughout Italy by means of merchant ships, and even after the first cases of plague in Italy, plague continued to be spread in favor of maximizing profits. Cholera was brought to Poland from the Asian border by Russian troop movements to fight the Polish uprising in Warsaw.

The year without a summer is the name given to 1816, which was unusually cold, especially in northeastern America and western and southern Europe. In the United States it was nicknamed "Eighteen hundred and froze to death," and in Germany it also became infamous as the misery year "Eighteen hundred and froze." Today, the eruption of the Indonesian volcano Tambora in April 1815 is considered to be the main cause, and volcanologists classify it as significantly stronger than the eruption of Mount Vesuvius in 79 AD and that of Krakatoa.

In 1920, the American climatologist William Jackson Humphreys found the first explanation for the "year without a summer." He attributed the climate change to the volcanic winter caused by the eruption of the Tambora volcano on the island of Sumbawa in what is now Indonesia. This had erupted in April 1815 with a magnitude of 7 on the Volcanic Explosivity Index and, in addition to about 150 km^3 of dust and ash, sulfur compounds estimated at a sulfur dioxide equivalent of 130 megatons were ejected high into the atmosphere, where they dispersed and settled like a veil around the entire globe. The cooling of the world's climate caused by the eruption continued until 1819.

The cold led to massive crop losses, so that famine broke out as a result of the lack of summer. In addition, floods led to over 100,000 deaths, so that migratory movements took place within the affected areas. Religious explanations and interpretations gained influence as people did not know how to explain this disaster.

The famine of 1817 gave rise to various measures to promote agriculture and, beyond that, to organizational reforms in the state sector, as well as to the foundation of charitable organizations. In hard-hit Württemberg, for example, King Wilhelm I initiated the founding of an agricultural association in 1817, whose central office organized an annual agricultural festival with competitions from 1818 onward, today's Cannstatt Folk Festival. His wife Katharina planned and directed the charity association, which, as a semi-governmental organization, assumed functions comparable to domestic development aid and famine and disaster relief from 1817 onward, and through which, in turn, the Württemberg Savings Bank was founded in 1818. Also in 1818, Wilhelm founded an agricultural teaching, experimental and model institute, today the University of Hohenheim.

The chemist Justus von Liebig was inspired by the memory of the famines to conduct his research on the conditions of plant growth. As a result of his research, mineral fertilization was introduced, which led to a significant increase in agricultural yields. According to the technology historian Hans-Erhard Lessing, the development of the draisine, the original bicycle, can be traced back to the death of horses as a result of the fodder shortage in 1816/17 following the Tambora eruption.

In the United States, crop failures caused many farming families from New England and other coastal states to move west to what was then the frontier, so that within a few years the states of Ohio, Indiana and Illinois were settled.

Using the Lisbon earthquake as an example, Alexander Kluge points to the drastic social and political changes that can result from a natural disaster.

"In Lisbon, the Jesuit order is banished, the Inquisition is pushed back, a piece of the mental Middle Ages is made known as useless. It is not only the writing Voltaire, it is the organizing force of the practitioner Pombal (from 1756 First Minister of Portugal, R.H.), who holds up a mirror to the thinking of the past. The natural disaster triggers a turning point, a departure. It is a catalyst in the process of enlightenment." (von Schirach, 2020, p. 51)

The Lisbon earthquake on November 1, 1755, along with a major fire and tsunami, almost completely destroyed the Portuguese capital of Lisbon. With

30,000 to 100,000 fatalities, this earthquake is one of the most devastating natural disasters in European history. It reached an estimated magnitude (magnitude) of about 8.5 to 9 on the moment magnitude scale. The epicenter is believed to be in the Atlantic Ocean about 200 km southwest of Cabo de São Vicente.

The earthquake had a significant impact on politics, culture and the sciences. It exacerbated domestic tensions in Portugal and led to a rupture in the country's colonial aspirations. Because of the great destruction, it triggered diverse discourses among Enlightenment philosophers; in particular, it raised anew the problem of theodicy, that is, the question of how a benevolent God could allow such evils in the world. This was further emphasized by the fact that the faithful in churches were destroyed, while the entertainment district was spared. The earthquake also had a significant impact on philosophically oriented discourses. Leibniz's thesis that we would live in the best of all possible worlds was thereby called into question.

"What had happened in Lisbon spoke against any "goodness of God", Voltaire in his Paris domicile not directly affected, nevertheless felt "agitated". A great city with a harbor, a thousand years old, must not be so mercilessly destroyed by the sea and an earth tremor as long as there is a self-confident humanity." (von Schirach, 2020, p. 50)

Voltaire declared war on nature in his poem on "Poème sur le désastre de Lisbonne." French President Macron also declared war on the virus last year. The war metaphor expresses the problem of mobilization.

References

Serres, M. (2016). *Auf wahre Information kommt es an.* https://taz.de/Philosoph-Michel-Serres-ueber-die-Moral/!5823030/ (translation by Rolf Hepp).

von Schirach, F. , & Kluge, A. (2020). *Trotzdem* (p. 50). Luchterhand (translation by Rolf Hepp).

Pandemic and Social Crisis in EU Policies: From the "Green New Deal" (2019) to the "Porto Social Summit" (2021). The Open Challenge of the Social Taxonomy

Marco Ricceri

1 Introduction

The profound and complex changes generated by the pandemic crisis in the social conditions of people—in the way of working, living, thinking, the systems of relationships, the life expectancy and ist prospects—require both new scientific cognitive approaches, and the definition of an integrated system of public policies and private actions aimed at organizing a new order based on social inclusion and effective human promotion; an operation made difficult by the fact that the structural crisis caused by the pandemic has created a general situation of uncertainty between the expectations of a return to the normal situation of the past and a widespread awareness that it will not be possible precisely due to the profound changes brought about by this crisis in our societies. The feeling and conditions of uncertainty widespread in society, with worryingly high risk of depression for many people, as evidenced for instance by Eurofound's annual e-surveys in the European system (see: Eurofound, Living, working and Covid-19 e-survey, 2022) have inevitably accentuated the phenomenon of social precariousness already widely present in our communities, caused mainly by the profound transformations taking place in the economy and in the world of work and, more generally, by the evident contradictions of a development model that

M. Ricceri (✉)
The Secretary General, EURISPES Institute, Rome, Italy
e-mail: eurispes.intl-dept@libero.it

R. D. Hepp (ed.), *Shifts and Reorientation Within the Social-Crisis and Catastrophe: Towards the Realization of Pandemic Epistemological Processes*, Prekarisierung und soziale Entkopplung – transdisziplinäre Studien,
https://doi.org/10.1007/978-3-658-43041-2_2

continues to generate profound inequalities between social groups; contradictions that the main international institutions and the states have undertaken to correct by building a new order based on the principles of sustainability (see the United Nations 2030 Agenda, 2015 and the consequent acts).

With regard to the spread of social precarity in our societies, it is useful to recall a further element that has long been well analyzed, highlighted and evaluated in particular by the scientific community. It concerns the fact that this negative process certainly originates, as we said, in the changes taking place in the world of work as well as in the growing economic inequalities that occur in our systems, but it is a process that progressively extends to involve the most diverse areas of community life, including the political one. The steps in this evolution are very clear: the job insecurity that arises in the world of work (employment–unemployment) gradually and quickly becomes professional precarity (due to the lack of skills and competences adequate to the new job needs) and therefore social precarity (due to inequalities in the levels of income and work opportunities) to the point of becoming psychological and existential precarity (due to the difficulty of formulating a life plan, create a family, having children, up to turning in on oneself, as shown by the many NEETs young people who decide not to work, not to get educated, and even to stop looking for a job) with the connected phenomena of disengagement in community life and absenteeism in politics as well as the negative instinctive reactions to official democratic choices of which widespread populisms are an expression. The pandemic crisis, with its uncertainty about future prospects, accentuates the spread of the process of social precarity and its evolution from job precarity to existential precarity; and this is the essential element to be placed at the center of scientific, economic, cultural and political analyses and evaluations.

2 EU Competencies and Principles in the Social and Labor Sphere

This article addresses these open problems by focusing attention on a specific aspect concerning the approach and policies approved by the EU on social issues, which include the processes of widespread precarity, with reference to the path taken in the period of pandemic crisis, from the presentation of the *Green New Deal* strategy (2019) to the decision to organize a special *Social Summit*, on 7–8 May 2021 in Porto (Portugal) with the precise aim of relaunching European social policy. A particular in-depth analysis is dedicated to the choices—or rather to the non-choices—that the EU has made in this period regarding the definition and application of the so called social taxonomy, i.e. that system of principles, indicators and criteria which, by integrating the action of the operators in the environmental dimension of development, plays a fundamental role in pursuing the objectives of sustainability.

In any case, before going into the merits of the evaluation of the recent Community initiatives in the field of social promotion, it is useful to recall two fundamental elements: a) the system of competences within which the EU can operate in the field of social and employment policies and b) the basic principles enshrined in the treaties that guide and regulate the entire European system, the EU and the member states. The reference is to the Lisbon Treaty, signed on 13 December 2007 and entered into force on 1 December 2009 (Treaty on European Union, Treaty on the functioning of the European Union, attached Protocols and Declarations).

2.1 The Competences of the EU

The Lisbon Treaty (2007)—i.e. the fundamental treaty that currently governs the Union—distinguishes very clearly between *exclusive competences* attributed directly to the full responsibility of the Union, *competing competences* in which the responsibilities for decisions and consequent acts are distributed between the EU and the member states called upon to collaborate with each other, and the responsibilities relating to *support, coordination and complement actions* that the European Union is required to carry out in relation to the primary action whose responsibility is attributed to the member states; in this case the principle of subsidiarity, which on the basis of the treaties inspires and governs the whole system of the Union, assumes a particularly important value.

The main element to keep in mind is the fact that in the field of social and labor policies the EU has not been attributed a primary, exclusive competence, a competence which has instead been maintained by the member states. On the basis of the treaties, therefore, the EU operates in this area within precise limits and only indirectly, with guidelines of a general nature, provisions and indications of an indicative but non-binding type, organizing and agreeing on plans, financial funds, support services to the initiative of the member states whose concrete implementation is, in any case, reserved to their full responsibility.

2.2 The Social Principles of the EU

As well known, the 2017 Lisbon Treaty profoundly reformed the structure of the Union and relaunched the integration process on new foundations, defining a very different system of governance, competences and commitments than in the past. It is the result of a tiring political compromise that has allowed the Union to emerge from the long phase of uncertainty following the referendum rejection of the previous treaty of 2004, "A Constitution for Europe", which set itself the ambitious goal—the dream of many pro-Europeans—to start a process of integration, also political-institutional, of the continent (towards the United States of Europe.

The interesting element to highlight concerns the fact that in the Lisbon Treaty the social topic has taken on a primary importance, on a par with the other topics relating to the progress and economic growth of the Union. Recognition of its importance is translated, concretely, into the affirmation of certain principles, a particular approach to development policies, the protection of rights and interests considered fundamental, the attribution of specific competences and responsibilities to the main social and territorial actors. This set of elements, of a general and particular order, characterizes the new orientation which is defined with a precise expression: the *social clause*. The social clause is, in short, the expression of a precise interpretation and vision of European society, of its development model, of the value of the needs expressed by citizens. This clause essentially defines the specific characteristics of the European social model and the elements of distinction from other models, such as, for example, the U.S. social model.

In practice, with the approval of the social clause, the Union has assumed the formal and fundamental commitment to evaluate and organize development policies in a way to promote, at the same time, a real social progress, of which it recognizes the value not only in terms of justice but also in terms of contribution to economic growth and the cohesion of the entire system. This is the constitutive element of the new phase of the integration process opened with the Lisbon Treaty of 2007, an element which objectively represents a real leap in quality compared to the previous phases.

The social change sanctioned and initiated by the treaty is explicitly mentioned in its reference principles. In fact, according to the treaty, the Union will have to operate according to the principles of *solidarity, subsidiarity, economic, social and territorial cohesion* (Lisbon Treaty 2007, articles 3–5) to promote *sustainable development based…on a highly competitive social market economy which aims at full employment and social progress* (Ibidem, art.3). The main tool for achieving this objective is the organization of a common *single market* (Ibidem, art.3), in which the four fundamental freedoms of free movement of people, goods, services and capital must be guaranteed. The methodological approach, of high political value, privileges, together with the collaboration between the member states, also the role of the social partners.

To strengthen this new approach, of great attention to social and labor issues, a decisive contribution comes, on the basis of the treaty, also from the recognition and inclusion of the *Charter of Fundamental Rights of the European Union*, with its principles that also regulate social dynamics, in the European law system. In this way, the Charter, solemnly proclaimed on 7 December 2000 by the European Parliament, the Council of Ministers and the European Commission, finally assumes a binding value: *The Union recognizes the rights, freedoms and principles set forth in the Charter of Fundamental Rights of the European Union ... It has the same legal value as the Treaties.* (Lisbon Treaty, 2007, art.6).

These are the main articles, on the basis of which the *social clause* has entered by right into the constitutive patrimony of the European Union. With regard to the possible interventions in the field of social promotion, the main innovations introduced by the treaty can be found in the following points: a) the reference to an economic model defined as the *social market economy*, on the basis of which the EU is committed to evaluating every initiative in favor of the market with the criterion of the social effects that such initiatives can produce. In this way, respect for the social clause has become a real constraint for all EU policies; b) the explicit reference to the objective of *full employment*, a statement of great significance because it commits the member states to a precise objective, which can also be measured on a statistical level. (in previous treaties, the expression used in this regard was quite different: in fact, the reference was made to a high level of employment); c) the reference to the role of the *dialogue between the social partners*, which has assumed much greater importance in the Lisbon Treaty than in previous treaties: *"the Union recognises and promotes the role of the social partners at its level, taking into account the diversity of national systems. It shall facilitate dialogue between the social partners, respecting their autonomy. The Tripartite Social Summit for Growth and Employment shall contribute to social dialogue". (TFEU, 2007, art.* n. 151,152,155).

With this, the Union entrusts the social partners with a very important role in pursuing the objectives of social promotion and employment. As we will examine later, for example, precisely in the period of the pandemic crisis, particularly in the years 2020–2021, the EU greatly intensified the use of this possibility, by promoting tripartite social summits for a more adequate definition of emergency and recovery policies.

3 The EU Recognition of the Primary Role of Social Policy: Value and Limits

In line with the international commitment to promote a new development model according to the principles of economic, social and environmental sustainability, between the end of 2019 and the beginning of 2020, i.e. before the spread of the pandemic crisis, the European Union has defined and officially presented its strategy on sustainable development as well as on strengthening social policy. The reference acts that mark the beginning of this new policy are the Communication on the "*European Green Deal*" (11 December 2019), the Communication on the "*2020 Annual Strategy on Sustainable Development*" (17 December 2019) and the Communication "*A Strong Social Europe for Just Transition*" (14 January 2020). These three documents mark the turning point to affirm—at least this is the explicit objective—a European policy oriented towards the construction of a new economic and social order. Their examination, like that of the political documents approved subsequently up to the *Social Summit* in Porto (Portugal) on 7–8 May 2021, offers useful knowledge elements to understand how the EU intends to tackle social problems, also with reference to the complex phenomenon of precarity.

The basic strategy defined in the *European Green Deal* has the objective of promoting a process of growth of the community system by applying the principle of sustainability in a perspective that sets specific objectives to be achieved in 2030 and 2050. The Green Deal—as illustrated in the document—is the way identified by the EU to participate and contribute to the achievement of the goals and tasks of the UN 2030 Agenda and at the same time affirm its competitive capacity on the international scene. The complex system of policies, plans, acts and regulations that derives from it and which was largely approved and applied in the immediately following period—an innovative process currently underway and destined to last over time—aims to profoundly affect and change the current European economic and productive system as well as the traditional way of living of our communities. This system has identified two main functional paths for achieving the objectives of sustainability in the so-called tween transition, green and digital, two areas of intervention identified as strategic for bringing out and spreading the benefits associated with the implementation of a new development model.

The need to accompany and integrate this complex process of structural reconversion of the European economic and productive system as well as its traditional consumption model with measures aimed at simultaneously strengthening its cohesion and social inclusion find precise indications in the specific document, already cited, "*A Strong Social Europe for Just Transitions*" (2020), which focuses attention above all on the following two main aspects: the changes in the world of work and the functionality of the related service structures that operate at European, national and regional level, from specialized agencies to public employment services (PES), which are also required in particular by the European Economic and Social Committee—EESC to extend their operational area to welfare services (EESC-SOC/620, 2019). Key tools of these new inclusive social policies are both the functionality and cooperation between these systems of employment services and the open and collaborative dialogue between the social partners; the latter, in particular, interpreted as an essential element to promote what is referred to as a socially responsible transition and, above all, to fully implement the commitments already approved by the highest European authorities and by the states with the document *European Pillar of Social Rights* (EPSR), solemnly proclamed and signed by the Council of the EU, the European Parliament and the Commission, and presented as a new constitutional charter aimed at support and qualify the European construction of the twenty-first century (European Council, Social Summit, Goeteborg, November 2017). It should be remembered that the document approved at the Goetoborg social summit referred to a previous communication presented on 26 April 2017 by the Commission in which the proposal relating, precisely, to the need to introduce the aforementioned European Pillar of Social Rights (EPSR) into the European system was articulated in 20 fundamental principles and rights to be applied in support of a renewed process of convergence towards better living and working conditions. These principles are divided into three categories: i) equal opportunities and access to the labor market, ii) fair working conditions, and iii) social protection and inclusion. The social pillar is accompanied by a social scoreboard for monitoring progress and by indicating a new approach to integrate social priorities into all policies, such as investment plans for the tween green and digital transitions.

With respect to the complex processes of the social precarity and its evolution from work and professional precarity to value, cultural, psychological and existential precarity, it is interesting to note how the EU indications and approach are essentially limited to addressing the problems connected to the transformations in progress in the world of work because in this reality the main cause of social insecurity is identified. Of course, the value of the influence of other factors, identified as the mega trends of our time, is clearly present in EU documents, from demographic processes to the complex impact of the digital revolution, just to name a few. An awareness that leads to affirm that in the European social model "technological innovation must go hand in hand with social innovation" (COM (2020)14Final). But the main approach, we repeat, is focused on transformations in the world of work to guarantee all European citizens equal opportunities to prosper and in this way correct the profound inequalities that persist in European society, a real brake on the possibilities of growth and a threat to the social cohesion of the whole EU system. In this context, the actions to promote with the aim to concretely implement the principles of the *European Pillar of Social Rights* are seen as functional to the construction of the social market economy, established in the treaties as a distinctive element of the Union compared to the models of other international realities.

4 Further Commitments of the European Parliament and the Commission in the Social Field

On 17 December 2020, at the end of a year of tragic pandemic crisis, the European Parliament approves the resolution "*A Strong Social Europe for Just Transitions*", (2020/2084(INI), which openly denounces a serious imbalance in European policy for sustainability that has neglected the social dimension of development: "so far priority has been assigned to economic and environmental sustainability" (Res.2084, 2020). And again: the implementation of the ten-year Lisbon strategy "*Europe 2020*", launched in 2010 and in force in the decade 2010–2020, "should have given greater priority to sustainability and inclusiveness, rather than growth" (Ibidem, 2020). The result of this unbalanced orientation of the policy pursued in particular after the financial crisis of 2008 onwards and the devastating effects of the pandemic crisis exploded at the beginning of 2020, have considerably worsened the social conditions of Europeans and created a very serious situation which, the EP resolution states, "puts in difficulty both the sustainability and the inclusiveness of growth and social cohesion" (Ibidem, 2020). The major negative aspects of the European situation concern "the growing intergenerational inequalities, the reduction of social, health, economic and environmental opportunities and resources, territorial disparities and unequal access to basic social and health services, to jobs and business opportunities as well as to social infrastructure" (Ibidem, 2020).

Faced with this situation, the corrective action to be promoted "consist of investments in people, aimed at improving their living conditions; whereas key policy areas for social investment include social security, health care, long-term care, education, housing, employment, justice and social services for disadvantaged groups; that well-designed social policies contribute strongly to sustainable development and growth, as well as protecting people from poverty and acting as economic stabilizers". (Ibidem, 2020). In this framework of social policies, priority importance is given to actions aimed at promoting "decent work and sustainable and inclusive labor markets" (Ibidem, 2020), to intervene with corrective measures to reduce "the increase in the number of workers with precarious and atypical forms of employment, of fictitious self-employed workers and workers with zero-hour contracts, even in national public administrations" (Ibidem, 2020). In this regard, the objective to pursue is that of "to work towards achieving the goal of eliminating involuntary temporary and part-time employment by 2030 and ensuring that 80% of the created jobs receive medium or high level remuneration and is concentrated in sustainable sectors"; as well as to "eliminate the practices of zero-hour contracts and fictitious self-employment" (Ibidem, 2020). Finally, the proposal presented by the European Parliament to the Commission and to the member states is characterized by three elements worthy of note: the first concerns the invitation to strengthen the traditional system of indicators applied in detecting the processes of change taking place in the world of work integrating it with "additional indicators" capable of analyzing and evaluating in a more appropriate way the transformations to be promoted in the social sphere for a truly balanced sustainable development. The second element concerns the "ambitious and mandatory" character that the new objectives of European social policy linked to sustainability should have. Finally, the third element concerns the need to refer to and integrate the "qunatitative and qualitative objectives' to be pursued" (Ibidem, 2020). These are all elements which, in fact, mark a turning point, also political, in the degree of awareness on the most appropriate ways of dealing in innovative terms with social and labor policies as well as to promote them in a consistent manner with the needs of the sustainability of the overall development process.

In essence, at the heart of the interventions proposed by the European Parliament for the organization of a true social Europe we find, therefore, the open problems of the world of work and employment and the commitment to promote sustainable labor markets, functional to the goal of "just transitions". In a subsequent resolution approved on 10 February 2021 in view of the European social summit scheduled for the following 7 May 2021 in Porto (Portugal), "*Reduction of inequalities with particular attention to working poverty*" (2019/2188 (INI)), the Parliament confirmed the value of this strategy: in fact it "considers of the utmost importance to ensure that the implementation of the Europe's recovery plan aims at eliminating poverty and socio-economic inequalities and is based on an effective mechanism with targets and parameters that allow for accurate measurement of all progress made" (Res.2188, 2021). Also noteworthy is the commitment, again confirmed, "in order to prevent the exploitation of workers in areas such as temporary work" (Ibidem, 2021) commonly recognized as one of the major elements at the origin of the spread of social precariousness.

Subsequent acts approved by the European Commission during 2021 are consistent with these European Parliament guidelines. "I believe—declared Commission President in front of the European Parliament on 20 January 2021—it is time to also adapt the social rulebook. A rulebook which ensures solidarity between generations. A rulebook that rewards entrepreneurs who take care of their employees. Which focuses on jobs and opens up on jobs and opens up new opportunities. Which puts skills, innovation and social protection on an equal footing". On 4 March 2021, the Commission made public the *Action Plan on the European Pillar of Social Rights* (COM(2021)102 Final), a document which provides the basic elements of the social summit planned for the May 7 2021. Essentially the document presents three points of notable novelty: the first concerns the function of social policy which is presented as an essential factor of economic growth; the second concerns the commitment to review together with the member states the body of laws on the subject to strengthen social rights and at the same time strengthen the European social dimension; the third point concerns the confirmation of the approach followed so far by the European Commission which identifies the true tools of social progress in the protection and promotion of work and employment. In this regard the Commission's documents indicates three precise goals to be achieved in Europe on 2030: "At least 78% of the population aged 20 to 64 should have in employment by 2030; … at least 60% of all adults should participate in training activities every year;… the number of people at risk of poverty or social exclusion should be reduced by at least 15 million by 2030" (COM(2021)102 Final). At the same time, in support of employment policies, on 4 March 2021, the Commission publishes the "*Recommendation on Active and Effective Support to Employment (EASE) following the COVID-19 crisis*" (Recommendation (EU) 2021/402).

5 Building the Social Europe: The New Role of Tripartite Social Summits

Created for the first time on 20 March 2003 on the basis of the conclusions of the Nice European Council (December 2000), which provided for an annual meeting of the social partners before the traditional spring European Council; of a subsequent communication by the European Commission (2002) on European Union Social Dialogue Process (COM(2002)341 final), and of a formal decision of the Council of 6 March 2003 (EU0303203F), the Tripartite Social

Summit for growth and employment is a forum for dialogue that replaced the previous permanent committee for employment with the aim of integrating the initiatives of the community authorities with the contribution of the social partners and consequently reinforcing the Lisbon strategy policies, "Europe 2020". The summits are generally attended at the presidential level by the European institutions (European Council, Commission, the head of state or government of the member state holding the EU presidency in rotation) and by representatives of the major social groups such as: BusinessEurope, which represents business federations in 34 European countries; European Trade Union Confederation (ETUC); SGI Europe (formerly known as CEEP); SMEunited (formerly known as European Association of Craft, Small and Medium-sized Enterprises (UEAPME); Eurocadres, the Council of European Professional and Managerial Staff. The main areas of discussion covered by the integrated concertation are essentially: macroeconomic issues; employment and social protection issues; the social dimension of the European integration process; education and training; progress achieved and ways to improve involvement of social partners in policies and reforms at national level. In 2007, the Tripartite Social Summit was officially included in the new EU treaty, the so called Lisbon Treaty, and recognized as one of the main tools for promoting social dialogue (art. 152 of the Treaty on the Functioning of the European Union—TFEU, 2007). Of great importance, also on a political level, was the organization of the Tripartite Social Summit sponsored by the Swedish government, which had the rotating presidency of the EU, on the occasion of the Goethenburg social summit, the "*Social summit for fair jobs and growth*", already mentioned, which on 17 November 2017 led to the proclamation of the "European Pillar of Social Rights"; in this way the involvement and active participation of the social partners in the definition of the document was guaranteed, a document which, with its twenty principles, currently constitutes the main reference for the labor and social policies of the Union.

But it is above all in the years 2020–2021, i.e. in the period of the serious crisis caused by the Covid 19 pandemic that the use of the Tripartite Social Summit initiative was intensified, surpassing the annual practice and allowing the community authorities to proceed expeditiously in defining of emergency and recovery policies also thanks to the elements collected, discussed and verified during the organic comparisons with the social partners. The tripartite social summits organized on 23 June and 14 October 2020 proved to be functional to this need. But there are also two other types of problems which in recent times have led the EU authorities to promote the initiative of the tripartite summits. These problems are related to the complexity of the processes related to the tween green and digital transition initiated by the EU to achieve the goals of sustainable development.

The implementation of such a strategy has revealed, for example, the need to give life to very widespread and profound productive restructurings, especially in the environmental and energy fields, a new situation which, in 2022, will also end up being affected by the negative effects of the—unimaginable—tragedy of the war in Ukraine, on the borders of the Union.

But also the progress of the digital revolution, with the radical and increasingly widespread changes induced in the world of work and in society, presents innovative elements such as to require increasingly close, integrated management between institutions and social partners, to identify the best solutions, starting with the regulatory system, designed to limit and reduce the negative effects and to bring out, on the contrary, the great positive potential of the digital processes. It is the need for the set-up of a participatory governance system with the sharing of addresses and responsibilities between the public and private actors, a solution repeatedly recommended by United Nations documents aimed at implementing the 2030 Agenda on sustainable development The practice of tripartite social summits intensified recently by the EU goes exactly in this direction. It is no coincidence that in the two tripartite summits of 2020, together with the priority problems linked to the Covid emergency and the recovery plans, those relating to digital innovations were also discussed: for instance, in the summit of 23 June 2021 which addressed the theme "Social Partners Autonomous Agreement on Digitalisation", and in the summit of 14 October 2021 which to the theme "job creation and social resilience" also added the following: "how can the recovery accelerate the digital transition and foster opportunities for workers and SMEs?".

The Tripartite Social Summit of 24 March 2021, called to face with the topic related to the overcoming the Covid emergency and improve recovery—"how to achieve a fair and sustainable recovery?"—also specifically addressed the underlying problem relating to the construction of social Europe; this with reference to the concrete implementation of the "European Pillar of Social Rights", an issue that the European Union has decided to address in a special social summit, scheduled by the Portuguese presidency in Porto in May 2021. A summit, we must add, in which, according to the President of the European Council, *Charles Michel*, the problem of social Europe will be placed "at the top of our political agenda" (C.Michel, declaration, 24.03.2021). In the same direction the declarations at the tripartite summit by the President of the European Commission, *Ursula von der Leyen*: "I strongly believe in the importance of social dialogue, which is a central pillar of our social market economy. The Porto Social Summit organized by the Portuguese Presidency will be an opportunity for everyone, trade unions and employers, but also civil society and institutions, to renew our joint commitment on the Social Europe we want to build." (U.v.d.Leyen, 24.03.3031)

6 The Porto Social Summit (2021)

"We underline the importance of European unity and solidarity in the fight against the COVID-19 pandemic. These values have defined the response of European citizens to this crisis and also lie at the heart of our common project and distinctive social model. More than ever, Europe must be the continent of social cohesion and prosperity. We reaffirm our pledge to work towards a social Europe". These words constitute the first point of the final declaration approved by the European Council, made up of the heads of state or government of the 27 EU member states, gathered at the social summit held on 7–8 May 2021 in Porto (Portugal). The summit was the event in which the major representatives of the European institutions and the social and civil society organizations, by deepening the discussion on three main targets to be achieved by 2030—employment, skills, social protection—have expressed the will to proceed in overcoming the pandemic crisis and in the recovery processes according to the principles and guidelines of the European social model, whose full centrality for the Union is reaffirmed. This is the most important political result achieved by the Porto Social Summit. Particularly significant are the terms used, for example, in the following points of the Final Declaration to illustrate the commitments relating to the promotion of an effective social policy consistent with the new European strategies for sustainability. Thus, for example, point 4 of the Declaration: "The European Pillar of Social Rights is a fundamental element of the recovery. Its implementation will strengthen the Union's drive towards a digital, green and fair transition and contribute to achieving upward social and economic convergence and addressing the demographic challenges. The social dimension, social dialogue and the active involvement of social partners have always been at the core of a highly competitive social market economy". Point 8 of the Declaration confirms the value of the opportunities linked to the new strategies for sustainability and at the same time the need to maintain a high level of attention and ensure an adequate intervention capacity to correct negative emergencies: "The green and digital transitions will bring enormous opportunities for European citizens but also many challenges, which will require more investment in education, vocational training, lifelong learning, upskilling and reskilling, so as to stimulate employment transitions towards sectors where there is a growing demand for labour. At the same time, changes linked to digitalisation, artificial intelligence, teleworking and the platform economy will require particular attention with a view to reinforcing workers' rights, social security systems and occupational health and safety". Finally, the Porto Declaration recognizes the value of the contribution of the social partners to opening up a completely new situation in the assessment of social progress. This is stated by the European Council in point 13: "We welcome, as another success of European social dialogue, that the European Social Partners have made a joint proposal for an alternative set of indicators to measure economic, social and environmental progress, supplementing GDP as welfare measure for inclusive and sustainable growth". In essence, with this article, the possibility is opened to evaluate the development path to be promoted in the next decade, its objectives and the related results actually achieved in both quantitative and qualitative terms. This last aspect of the approach to the dynamics of development objectively constitutes an element of considerable political, cultural and scientific innovation which enters the standards of European documents. It would be the first step, we can add, to affirm in the European system the theoretical and practical guidelines linked to the social quality of development; to open up a decidedly different scenario from the one we have had so far.

The commitments defined and assumed by the highest representatives of the Union at the Porto Social Summit in 2021 are therefore very clear, as is the catchword chosen by the current president of the European Council, the Portuguese Andrea Costa, promoter of the initiative: " Time to deliver". (A.Costa, Porto Summit, 2021)

7 Sustainable Development and the Open Challenge of Social Taxonomy

The concrete contribution of the European Union to achieving the sustainability objectives of the 2030 Agenda, witnessed by the approval of the Green Deal strategy (2019) and numerous consequent acts aimed at implementing coherent plans and initiatives in the most diverse development areas, has a fundamental point of reference in the definition of a precise system of guidelines, targets and indicators which translate the complex system promoted the United Nations within the EU. This is the so-called European taxonomy defined, approved and applied with a community regulation, therefore with an immediately enforceable regulatory act, which precisely indicates to operators in finance and productive activities, industry and services, the objectives of change to be pursued in order to take and follow the path of a different, in fact, sustainable development model. The European taxonomy is therefore the tool with which the EU promotes the Green Deal, first of all with specific reference to the so called green economy, and in the same time the convergence of its economic and productive system on the objectives indicated by the United Nations 2030 Agenda. Obviously, it deals with a complex process, started in 2020, also with the modification and updating of previous community provisions, a process still ongoing in 2022, destined in any case to be enriched with further elements.

The fundamental law provision of this step forward, made by the EU in the period 2020–2021 with the approval and entry into force of various acts aimed at such purpose, is constituted by the European Taxonomy Regulation (EC, 2020/852) which defines the terms of economic activities to be considered as eco-compatible. The document presents a complex system of conditionalities and precise indicators that companies are obliged to respect in their organizational, productive and restructuring processes connected with the transition needs; all this in order to be considered as subjects who actually operate according to the principles and objectives summarized in the acronym ESG (Environment, Social, Governance); that is, as subjects who, in pursuing their profit objectives, operate at the same time with a sense of responsibility and attention to the positive and negative implications that their investments and initiatives have on the environment, on society and on respect for the expectations of different stakeholders (the last deals with the governance, which essentially refers to the decision and management mechanisms applied by a company).

7.1 The Environmental Taxonomy

In this regard, it is appropriate to underline an essential fact: the one approved and made executive by the EU bodies is also commonly defined with the terminology Environmental Taxonomy or Green Taxonomy, because the system of guidelines, rules and indicators that companies are required to apply concerns above all the impact of their activity on the environment. In this field of interventions, the indications and prescriptions are very punctual and precise. On the contrary, much more general and generic are the indications relating to the social impact of business activity. That's the reason why the EU has launched a specific process for solving the open problems relating to an adequate regulation of the activities that intervene in the social dimension of development, a process aimed at defining and approving a social taxonomy to be applied in parallel to the aforementioned green taxonomy in the future. Let's say right away that the elaboration of this social taxonomy presents great difficulties relating, for example, to the definition itself and to the implications of what is meant by social, in particular when social promotion is linked to the construction of a development model, different from the one pursued up to now, based more on the quality than on the quantity of growth, precisely a sustainable model. It deals with the great open problem of this transition phase that requires everyone, from the scientific world to economic operators, from public decision makers to representatives of civil society organizations, to be available for a sincere discussion for the identification of possible and valid theoretical and practices paths aimed precisely at the elaboration of a valid and shared social taxonomy. A taxonomy, we add, in which the complex issues of social precariousness must find space.

The EU Taxonomy Regulation mainly refers to three regulations approved in 2020–2021, i.e. to acts with the force of law immediately applicable throughout the Community system: the aforementioned EU Regulation 2020/852; a subsequent EU Delegated Regulation 2021/2139 which supplements the previous one and sets out the technical evaluation criteria to be used in the context of a list of around one hundred production activities; the EU Regulation 2021/2178, also with further additions to previous acts, which provides indications on the way in which finance and economic operators must carry out non-financial reporting of their activities, highlighting their sustainable nature, that is with references to their impact on the environment and society. The following measures intervene in particular on this specific aspect of non-financial reporting: "*The Sustainable Finance Disclosure Regulation–SFDR*" of 2019 (Regulation (EU2019/2088) and the "*Corporate Sustainability Reporting Directive—CSRD*" (2021) on corporate sustainability reporting which substantially replace the previous directive on "Non -financial reporting—NFRD" n.95 of 2014; and, under discussion on 2022, the Directive proposal on "*Corporate Sustainability Due Diligence and amending Directive (EU) 2019/1937*" announced in 2021 and officially presented by the European Commission on 23.02.2022 (COM(2022) 71Final.

At the basis of these regulations we find the EU's need, in line with the Green Deal strategy, to direct capital flows towards sustainable investments; to increase investor confidence and make them more aware of the environmental impacts of these financial or corporate bonds that they may have; to create visibility and address concerns related to greenwashing which consists of gaining an unfair competitive advantage by marketing a financial product as eco-sustainable even though it does not meet basic environmental standards. In essence, these regulations are aimed at industrial or service companies, the world of credit and investors who have to decide where to use their financial resources. These subjects can also be small investors and small savers who are granted the right to have transparent information about the actual sustainability of the investment they are making. In particular, with reference to the non-financial reporting to which economic operators are required, the documents to be presented to the competent authorities must illustrate that the investment and related activity contribute substantially to the achievement of one or more of the objectives of environmental sustainability, that it does not cause significant harm to the environment, that complies with the technical indications provided by the European Commission, and, finally, that respects the safeguarding of the fundamental rights of workers.

In particular, the framework of objectives referred to by the complex system of classification, indicators and the technical evaluation criteria elaborated by the European Commission is very clear and well defined. The framework of the objectives is contained in Annexes I and II of the regulation which entered into force in 2021 (EU Regulation 2021/2139); it makes it possible to evaluate, in practice, whether and how a company carries out operations in a manner consistent with the needs of sustainability; what is its substantial contribution, direct or indirect, to this end; what negative impacts its activity can have on the environment, in the short and long term.

The six environmental and climate objectives of the aforementioned EU regulation are as follows:

* mitigation of climate change: the intervention is on the causes of gas emissions greenhouse, therefore above all CO2, methane, hydrofluorocarbons
* adaptation to climate change: the intervention is on the effects of gas emissions greenhouse;
* sustainable use and protection of water and marine resources;
* the transition to a circular economy, i.e. the reduction of natural resources at the source, reuse, recycling, waste reduction, the use of secondary raw materials (i.e. obtained from recycling), the reduction of the use of dangerous substances and the reduction of incineration;
* the reduction of soil, air and water pollution not caused by greenhouse gases;
* the protection and restoration of biodiversity and ecosystems; forest management and sustainable agriculture.

Faced with these provisions, it is therefore possible to state that overall the EU taxonomy has so far sufficiently defined a system of classification of economic and productive activities in relation to their environmental impact; a system well organized in its general and specific objectives, the indicators and criteria to be applied in the evaluation processes, the conditions to be met in order to operate in transparency and to provide the community with adequate information on the initiatives undertaken by the economic operators and the actual results achieved.

7.2 The Social Taxonomy

But, as mentioned above, the path indicated for the construction of a truly sustainable development model, well balanced in its quantitative and qualitative aspects, according to the United Nations 2030 Agenda strategy, implemented and confirmed by the European Green Deal, requires states and operators to proceed in parallel in the three main dimensions of growth, namely the economic, environmental and social dimensions. The real open problem, in the context of which adequate solutions can also be found to at least reduce and limit the serious conditions of precariousness widespread in our societies, concerns precisely the insufficient answers given so far at an international and European level precisely in the social dimension of development.

It is true that the environmental taxonomy approved by the EU contains some elements which must induce economic operators to carefully consider also some social effects of their activity, in particular regarding the rights and conditions of workers and to illustrate in their non-financial reports to the authorities the results actually achieved. This applies, for example, to the minimum safeguards that operators are required to ensure in carrying out their sustainable economic activities with reference to the main international instruments such as: the "International Bill of Human Rights" (1966) (composed by the "Universal Declaration of Human Rights" UDHR, 1948; the "UN Covenants on Civil and Political Rights", ICCPR, 1966; and the "Economic, Social and Cultural Rights", ICESCR,1966); the International Labor Organization—ILO "Declaration on Fundamental Rights and Principles at Work" (1998, amended in 2022); the "UN Guiding Principles on Business and Human Rights-UNGPs" (2011); the OECD "Guidelines for Multinational Enterprises-MNEs" (2011). Further elements of the current European taxonomy that also refer to the social impact of the activities undertaken by operators to protect the environment are contained in the European acts and documents relating to "Corporate Sustainability Reporting—CSRD" (2021), the "Sustainable Finance Disclosures Regulation" (2019), the "Sustainable Corporate Governance –SCG" (2020). But beyond these very circumscribed and limited references to specific problems, the real fact is that an organic social taxonomy within the EU is still to be elaborated. Bridging this serious gap as a matter of urgency is a great open challenge for everyone: European and national authorities (who have primary competence in social matters), social partners, the scientific community; a challenge that requires highly integrated action at the various levels of intervention, which concerns the possibility of proceeding in an organic and effective way in the construction of a sustainable development model, determining the success or otherwise of the EU strategy;

which finally allows for the concrete follow-up to the commitment repeatedly proclaimed in many authoritative forums to strengthen the social dimension of the EU.

On 15 October 2020, the Commission inaugurated the first session of "*Platform on Sustainable Finance*", a consultative body, made up of 57 members and 11 observers, experts from the most diverse disciplines and sectors of activity, from industry, academia, civil society, established on the basis of art. 20 of the Taxonomy Regulation with the task of assisting the Commission in the elaboration of the European taxonomy. In the final report published in February 2022 and elaborated after extensive consultation with external subjects and a great in-depth work, the subgroup in charge to define the structure, criteria and indicators of the social taxonomy has provided important indications on the fixed points to be taken as basic references and on the path to be taken to arrive at the definition of a truly adequate social taxonomy, coherent and functional with the needs of sustainable development; but the subgroup also clearly outlined the difficulties that still remain to be overcome and the knots that should be resolved both in the theoretical and in the practical approach to the problems of the social dimension of growth.

The main key points highlighted in the report are the following:

**The environmental taxonomy already developed and applied within the EU can be taken as a model for the social taxonomy.*

The Commission itself recommends proceeding in this direction given the good overall organization of the environmental taxonomy, its functionality in supporting the choices of operators, the considerable recognition obtained both within and outside the EU. "Keeping the social taxonomy in line with the design of the environmental taxonomy might therefore help with global market acceptance and understanding" (Platform on Sustainable Finance, Final Report on Social Taxonomy, 2022, p. 29). It would also support the work of the "International Platform on Sustainable Finance", which is currently developing a 'common ground taxonomy' to highlight commonalities between existing taxonomies. "Therefore, as a starting point—the report states -, a social taxonomy should follow the steps of the environmental taxonomy by: i) first setting social objectives; ii) then setting out the substantial contributions that can achieve these objectives; and finally iii) drawing up criteria that apply the principle of not doing any significant harm, so that contributing to achieving one objective is not detrimental to the others. Ultimately, the need for minimum environmental safeguards will have to be considered, depending on whether the social and environmental taxonomies will be combined or will remain separate". (Ibidem, p. 29)

**The foundations of social taxonomy are established by international principles and standards* which the report expressly refers to and which are partly a reference also for environmental taxonomy (already partially mentioned above): the Universal Declaration of Human Rights, the International Covenant on Economic, Social and Cultural Rights, the International Covenant on Civil and Political Rights, the ILO Declaration on Fundamental Principles and Rights at Work, the ILO Tripartite Declaration of Principles concerning Multinational Enterprises and Social Policy, the European Convention on Human Rights, the European Social Charter, the Charter of Fundamental Rights of the European Union, the European pillar of social rights, the SDGs, the Guiding Principles on Business and Human Rights—UNGPs, the UN Global Compact, the OECD guidelines for Multinational Enterprises MNEs.

"These documents—the report states—cover a wide range of social topics that can be brought within the scope of the social taxonomy including: labour rights, social protection and inclusion, non-discrimination, the right to health care, housing, education (including professional training) and food, assistance in the event of unemployment or self-employment, consumer protection, peaceful and inclusive societies, the fight against corruption and tax evasion". (Ibidem, p. 32)

**The proposal of three social groups and three reference objectives.*

In organizing the social taxonomy, the report proposes to concentrate the complex scheme of this tool on three main groups of stakeholders—*workers, consumers, communities and society*—and to define the criteria and indicators in relation to the following three fundamental objectives:

Decent Work (Including Value-Chain Workers)

"This objective focuses on people in their working lives or as workers. The formulation of this objective acknowledges the helpful role of the decent-work agenda spearheaded by the International Labour Organization. The four pillars of the decent-work agenda are: employment creation, social protection, rights at work and social dialogue. This objective would include sub-objectives that emphasise some of these four pillar. Because it also relates to the just transition, this objective would also reflect employment generation for certain groups of people (such as those left unemployed by the closure of polluting industries)". (Ibidem, p. 34)

Adequate Living Standards and Wellbeing for End-Users

"This objective focuses on people in their role as end-users of certain products and services that either pose heightened health or safety risks or that have the potential to help people to meet basic human needs. The sub-objectives will emphasise aspects related to consumer protection and the realisation of economic and social rights such as the right to health, food, housing and education". (Ibidem, p. 34)

Inclusive and Sustainable Communities and Societies
"This objective will emphasise respecting and supporting human rights by paying attention to the impacts of activities on communities and the wider society. It will achieve this by: i) addressing and avoiding negative impacts; and ii) making basic economic infrastructure available to certain target groups. This objective focuses on people in their role as members of communities. The sub-objectives under this objective will emphasise issues such as: i) land rights; ii) indigenous people's rights; iii) human-rights defenders; and iv) improving/maintaining the accessibility and availability of basic economic infrastructure and services like clean electricity and water for certain vulnerable groups or groups in need". (Ibidem, p. 34)

7.3 The Social Taxonomy and the Open Question of Ist Scientific Foundations

Compared to these well-identified and acquired elements and to the following very detailed and articulated scheme on the basis of which the proposal of the social taxonomy is organized, the report nevertheless presents a decidedly open fundamental question mark on which ultimately the value or otherwise of the whole initiative depends: and, we may add, also the possibility of intervening on the complex phenomenon of social precariousness. The point concerns the diversity of scientific foundations between environmental taxonomy and social taxonomy.

"The foundations of the environmental taxonomy are natural science and international frameworks such as the Paris Agreement. Criteria for the environmental taxonomy were generally developed on the basis of scientifically validated research results. A social taxonomy, however, cannot be based on science in the same way. While the science behind climate change gives clear answers on CO_2 reduction requirements, science is not systematically able to play such a role for social factors. And although there is abundant research on social phenomena within social sciences that can influence the development of a social taxonomy, science cannot play the same role here as it does in the environmental taxonomy...Finally, it might be more difficult—at least initially—to develop quantifiable criteria for a social taxonomy than for an environmental taxonomy.

This is because, for environmental topics (and climate-change mitigation in particular), scientific research makes it possible to attach highly relevant quantitative criteria to economic activities. However, social sustainability is at the moment often described in more qualitative terms. However, —the report adds—promising developments are occurring in the field of quantifiable social data. For example, the EU *acquis* in the social fields gives clear policy and legislative references/ indicators that measure social impact. More recently, the EU's 'social scoreboard' represents relevant examples and recommendations for implementing the 20 principles of the European pillar of social rights, and contains a set of indicators of impact. These examples, recommendations and indicators can be used in the EU social taxonomy to measure access to social protection". (Ibidem, p. 30).

In this situation, faced with the limits and insufficiencies of the scientific foundations that the group of European experts has highlighted in the social analysis aimed at sustainable development, the proposed solution is that in any case the social taxonomy "has to be based on international authoritative standards of topical relevance such as the International Bill of Human Rights" (Ibidem, p. 7); this is unlike environmental taxonomy which can refer to science-based goals and criteria.

The report, of which we have recalled some essential passages, has the value of a proposal from the group of high-level experts to the European Commission, a proposal aimed at defining a social taxonomy that can operate in parallel with the environmental taxonomy, already approved and in force as a legal act. The question that arises spontaneously is the following: is this first approach defined by the experts sufficient to achieve the objective of a valid definition of the social taxonomy to be applied in the European system? Do the qualitative criteria with which social phenomena are often described and evaluated really have a weak scientific foundation and, consequently, constitute a limit to the elaboration of this essential tool for sustainability? And how to justify this limit with respect to the strategic objective of sustainability which refers to the transition from a model based on quality rather than quantity of development? And, again: how to deal with a social taxonomy of a phenomenon as complex as that of social precariousness articulated in its economic, cultural, existential aspects? All these are questions that arise spontaneously in the face of the statements of this report by the community experts—really very honest and clear—on the difficulties and limits they have found in the definition of the social taxonomy.

For the scientific community, therefore, this report opens up a precise task: to clarify the terms of the social quality of development and, in particular, that expressions such as good health, well-being, social inclusion, social cohesion are not only conceptual expressions, with uncertain scientific foundations, but phenomena and processes that can be well defined and included in a valid systemic classification, evaluated and measured on the basis of precise basic indicators, appropriately integrated with each other.

Closing Remarks

The lesson we can draw from the illustration of European social policies adopted in the first and a half year of the pandemic crisis allows us to highlight three main elements.

The first concerns the turning point made by the European authorities in the explicit recognition of the value of social policy as a primary factor in a just and balanced development. The need to operate in a coherent way with the internationally approved guidelines for sustainability and to tackle the tragic effects of the pandemic with effective recovery measures has led the EU to change its traditional approach to social policy, removing it from that secondary position into which it has been relegated and lived for many years.

The second element concerns the European authorities' assessment of social precarity which essentially focuses on the problems raised by the dynamics of the world of work. Few and limited to this area are the references to the diffusion of social precarity in official European documents, as we have seen in the illustrative path made in this article. In practice, in these official political acts there are no references to the complexity and riskiness of the diffusion of value, cultural, psychological, existential precarity, whose negativity for human dignity as well as for the social cohesion of our systems has long been highlighted in a particular way by the scientific community. Consequently, we are facing with a very serious open problem which is certainly destined to produce deleterious effects on the very stability of democratic systems. Taking note of it and addressing it adequately is first of all an ethical duty for everyone, first of all, for the ruling class as a whole and specifically for those responsible for public decision-makers.

The third element concerns the will and ability of the European system to promote concrete initiatives that are truly consistent with the approach and implications of the strategy aimed at building a sustainable development model. The commitment repeatedly affirmed and shared in the most authoritative institutions, public and private, to proceed in a balanced way in the three dimensions of economic, environmental and social growth cannot be pursued in a partial way; it would be a contradiction capable of jeopardizing the whole set of sustainability efforts carried out in Europe. The reference is to the accumulated delays in the definition and application of an adequate system of social taxonomy, to be integrated in its setting and application with the already launched environmental taxonomy, in order to guide and promote the choices of the main development players in a truly organic way towards an innovative scenario defined by precise parameters of quality, as well as quantity.

The elaboration and entry into force of the social taxonomy is the real test that is currently faced by the European authorities, the member states, the social partners. Such a step forward is objectively essential to affirm, together with the principles of sustainability, the distinctive value of the European model as a social market economy, enshrined in the 2007 treaty, and the primary role of social policy which has been widely recognized at the top level of European authorities from 2017 onwards.

We have definitely entered a phase in which it is more necessary and urgent than ever to give a precise value to the keywords, already mentioned, with which the former president of the European Council, the Portuguese Andrea Costa, promoted the Porto social summit in 2021: "Time to deliver" (A.Costa, 2021). The final reflection concerns precisely the possibility or not of such an advance of the European system.

Further Reading

Committee of the Regions CoR. (2021). *Press release on the European pillar of social rights* (Vol. 4).

EU Social Summit 21. (2021, May 7). *Porto Social Commitment.*

ETUC, Business Europe, Sgi Europe, Sme United. (2021, March 2021). *Supplementing GDP as welfare measure.* Proposed joint list by the European Social Partners.

Eurofound. (2022). *Fifth round of the Living, working and COVID-19 e-survey: Living in a new era of uncertainty.* EF/22/042/EN. https://www.eurofound.europa.eu/topic/covid-19

European Economic and Social Committee-EESC. (2019, February 20). *The new role of Public Employment Services in the framework of the implementation of the European Pillar of Social Rights.* Opinion, SOC/620.

European Commission. (2010, March 3). *"Europe 2020". A 10-year strategy in force in the decade 2010–2020 for "smart, sustainable, inclusive growth".* Communication (COM(2010) 2020 final).

European Commission. (2013, June 26). *Directive 2013/34/EU of the European Parliament and the Council on the Annual financial statements, consolidated financial statements and related reports of certain types of undertakings, amending Directive 2006/43/EC of the European Parliament and of the Council and repealing Council Directives 78/660/EEC and 83/349/EEC, EUR-Lex-32013L0034.*

European Commission. (2014, November 15). *Non financial Reporting Directive—NFRD (2014/95/EU), amending Directive 2013/34/EU as regards disclosure of non-financial and diversity information by certain large undertakings and groups,* OJ L 330.

European Commission. (2017). *The European Pillar of Social Rights.* Publication Office KA-05-17 081-EN-NE.
European Commission. (2017). *Reflection paper on the social dimension of Europe.* COM, p. 206.
European Commission. (2018, March 8). *Action Plan: Financing Sustainable Growth.* Communication from the Commission to the European Parliament, the European Council, the Council, the European Economic and Social Committee and the Committee of the Regions, COM/2018/097 final.
European Commission. (2019, December 9). *Regulation (EU) 2019/2088 of the European Parliament and of the Council of 27 November 2019 on sustainability-related disclosures in the financial services sector (SFDR),* OJ L 317.
European Commission. (2019, December 11). *The European Green Deal.* Communication COM 2019-640.
European Commission. (2019, December 17). *Annual sustainable growth strategy 2020,* Communication, COM 650-final.
European Commission. (2020). *Employment and Social Developments in Europe 2020.* Report. https://ec.europa.eu/social/main.jsp?catId=738&langId=en&pubId=8342.
European Commission. (2020). *Communication to the European Parliament and the Council on the EU Action Plan on Human Rights and Democracy 2020–2024* (JOIN/2020/5 final).
European Commission. (2020, January 14). *A strong social Europe for just transitions.* Communication (COM (2020)14Final.
European Commission. (2020). *Employment and Social Developments in Europe* report https://ec.europa.eu/social/main.jsp?catId=738&langId=en&pubId=8342&furtherPubs=yes
European Commission, Technical Expert Group on Sustainable Finance. (2020, March 2020). *Taxonomy: Final report.*
European Commission. (2020, May 27). Europe's moment: Repair and prepare for the next generation, communication. *"Next Generation EU (NGEU)"*, COM(2020) 456 final.
European Commission. (2020, June 22). *Regulation (EU) 2020/852 of the European Parliament and of the Council of 18 June 2020 on the establishment of a framework to facilitate sustainable investment, and amending Regulation* (EU) 2019/2088, OJ L 198, (Taxonomy Regulation).
European Commission. (2020, September 17). *Annual Sustainable Growth Strategy 2021, Communication.* COM(2020)575final.
European Commission. (2020). *Communication to the European Parliament, the Council, the European Economic and Social Committee and the Committee of the Regions on A new Circular Economy Action Plan for a cleaner and more competitive Europe* (COM/2020/98 final).
European Commission. (2021, March 4). *Action plan on the pillar European Social Rights.* COM (2021)102Final.
European Commission. (2021, March 4). *Action plan on the pillar European Social Rights.* COM (2021) 102Final, Annex.1.
European Commission. (2021, March 4). *Recommendation on active effective support to employment following the COVID-19 crisis (EASE).* Recommendation 2021/402.

European Commission. (2021, April 24). *Proposal for a Directive of the European Parliament and of the Council amending Directive 2013/34/EU, Directive 2004/109/EC, Directive 2006/43/EC and Regulation (EU) No 537/2014, as regards corporate sustainability reporting*. COM/2021/189 final.

European Commission. (2021, June). Employment and Social Developments in Europe 2021. *Annual Review*.

European Commission. (2021, July 6). *Strategy for Financing the Transition to a Sustainable Economy*. Communication from the Commission to the European Parliament, the European Council, the Council, the European Economic and Social Committee and the Committee of the Regions, COM/2021/390 final.

European Commission. (2021, June 4). *EU Delegated Regulation 2021/2139*, supplementing Regulation (EU) 2020/852 of the European Parliament and of the Council. Attachments I and II. https://eur-lex.europa.eu/eli/reg_del/2021/2139/oj

European Commission. (2021, July 6). *EU Delegated Regulation 2021/2178* supplementing Regulation (EU) 2020/852 of the European Parliament and of the Council.

European Commission. (2021). *Corporate Sustainability Reporting Directive—CSRD* (SWD/2021/150 final).

European Commission. (2021, December 1). *Commission Delegated Regulation (EU) 2021/2105 supplementing Regulation (EU) 2021/241 of the European Parliament and of the Council establishing the Recovery and Resilience Facility by defining a methodology for reporting social expenditure*. Official Journal of the European Union, L 429.

European Commission, Platform on Sustainable Finance. (2022, February 23). *Final Report on Social Taxonomy*, European Commission: *Proposal for a Directive on corporate sustainability due diligence*, Proposal to the European Parliament and the Council, (COM2022)71Final).

European Commission. (2022). *Communication to the European Parliament, the Council and the European Economic and Social Committee on decent work worldwide for a global just transition and a sustainable recovery*, COM(2022) 66 final.

European Council. (2020, December 1). *Conclusions on Human Rights and Decent Work in Global Supply Chains* (13512/20).

European Council. (2021, May 8). *The Porto Declaration*, European Social Summit, High-Level Conference, Porto. www.2021portugal.eu/en/porto-social-summit

European Parliament. (2020, December 17). *A strong social europe forjust transitions*, Resolution, (2020/2084 (INI).

European Parliament. (2021, February 10). *Reduction of inequalities with particular attention to working poverty*, Resolution (2019/2188 (INI)).

European Parliament. (2021). Resolution with *recommendations to the Commission on corporate due diligence and corporate accountability* (2020/2129(INL), 10.03.2021. https://oeil.secure.europarl.europa.eu/oeil/popups/ficheprocedure.do?lang=en&reference=2020/2129(INL)

European Parliament. (2022). Proposal for a directive of the European Parliament and of the Council on *Corporate Sustainability Due Diligence* and amending Directive (EU)2019/1937 (COM(2022)0071—C9-0050/2022—2022/0051(COD)), 7.11.2022.

European Parliament. (2022, November 10). *New EU sustainability reporting rules for multinationals*. Resolution

European Union. (2007). *Treaty on European Union (TEU): Art.3 Social Market Economy*, Lisbon OJ C306/2, 13.12.2007.
European Union. (2007). *Treaty on the Functioning of the European Union (TFEU)*, Consolidated version, 2008,. *The role of Social Dialogue*, Articles n. 151,152,155, Lisbon 13 December 2007, OJ 2008/C 115/01, May 9, 2008.
European Union—Tripartite Social Summit. (2020, June 19–23). *Contribution of the social partners to relaunching growth and employment in the aftermath of COVID*.
European Union—Tripartite Social Summit. (2020, October 14). *Implementing together an inclusive economic and social recovery in Europe*.
European Union—Tripartite Social Summit. (2021, March 24). *How to achieve a fair and sustainable Recovery*.
International Labour Organisation—ILO. (2017). *Tripartite Declaration of Principles concerning Multinational Enterprises and Social Policy* (5th ed.). https://www.ilo.org/empent/Publications/WCMS_094386/lang--en/index.htm
Organisation for Economic Co-operation and Development-OECD (2011): *Guidelines for Multinational Enterprises*. https://doi.org/10.1787/9789264115415-en, with set of recommendations on responsible business conduct. http://mneguidelines.oecd.org/guidelines/
Organisation for Economic Co-operation and Development-OECD. (2018). *Due Diligence Guidance for Responsible Business Conduct*; OECD *sectoral guidance*. https://www.oecd.org/investment/due-diligence-guidance-for-responsible-business-conduct.htm
Organisation for Economic Co-operation and Development-OECD. (2020): *Supporting people and companies to deal with the COVID-19 virus: Options for an immediate employment and social-policy response*. OECD Policy Responses to Coronavirus (COVID-19).
United Nations (UN). (2011). *Guiding principles on business and human rights: Implementing the United Nations 'Protect, Respect and Remedy' Framework*". https://www.ohchr.org/Documents/Publications/GuidingPrinciplesBusinessHR_EN.pdf
United Nations—UN. (2015). *Resolution, Transforming our world: The 2030 Agenda for Sustainable Development*.
United Nations—UN. (2022). The *Sustainable Development Goals Report 2022*. UNDESA.

Websites

Council of Europe: European Convention on Human Rights (3 Sept. 1953). https://www.echr.coe.int/documents/convention_eng.pdf
Council of Europe: European Social Charter. (1961; revisited 1996). https://www.coe.int/en/web/european-social-charter.
European Union: Charter of Fundamental Rights (Lisbon Treaty, 2007). https://ec.europa.eu/info/aid-development-cooperation-fundamental-rights/your-rights-eu/eu-charter-fundamental-rights_en
European Union: European Pillar of Social Rghts—Associated Action Plan (2017). https://ec.europa.eu/info/strategy/priorities-2019-2024/economy-works-people/jobs-growth-and-investment/european-pillar-social-rights/european-pillar-social-rights-20-principles_en

International Labour Organization (ILO) (2015). *Guidelines for a just transition towards environmentally sustainable economies and societies for all.* http://www.ilo.org/wcmsp5/groups/public/---ed_emp/---emp_ent/documents/publication/wcms_432859.pdf

United Nations (UN): UN Global Compact 2017. *Blueprint for Business Leadership on the SDG, A principles based approach 2017.* https://d306pr3pise04h.cloudfront.net/docs/publications%2FBlueprint-for-Business-Leadership-on-the-SDGs.pdf

New Forms of Social Support for Russian Population During the COVID-19 Coronavirus Pandemic

Vyacheslav Bobkov, Elena Odintsova, and Igor Shichkin

The socio-economic consequences of the COVID-19 pandemic in the world have manifested themselves in a significant increase in morbidity, unemployment, poverty and social inequity. Mortality also increased. In this regard, many national governments have implemented a set of financial, monetary and social policy measures aimed at minimizing the negative effects of social risks.

In 2020 during the acute phase of COVID-19 pandemic, the Russian Government took a number of important measures in order to support certain categories of citizens and businesses. As a result, it became possible to restrain the decline of GDP. It decreased by 4% compared with 2019 which is significantly lower than in most countries.

First of all, the amount of unemployment benefits were paid in accordance with the regional subsistence minimum. The unemployed people who have minor children in their households, were given additional payments of 3 thousand rubles (about $ 40) on a regular basis. Moreover, payments of 10 thousand rubles (about

V. Bobkov (✉) · E. Odintsova
Institute of Economics, Russian Academy of Sciences, Moscow, Russia
e-mail: bobkovvn@mail.ru

E. Odintsova
e-mail: odin_ev@mail.ru

I. Shichkin
Plekhanov Russian University of Economics, Moscow, Russia

R. D. Hepp (ed.), *Shifts and Reorientation Within the Social-Crisis and Catastrophe: Towards the Realization of Pandemic Epistemological Processes*, Prekarisierung und soziale Entkopplung – transdisziplinäre Studien,
https://doi.org/10.1007/978-3-658-43041-2_3

$ 134) were made to all families with children under 16 years old during several month.

Some regions adopted their own additional programs to support citizens. So in the Moscow region, persons aged 65 and over, and residents suffering from certain chronic diseases, observing the regime of self-isolation received a lump sum payment of 3,000 rubles. ($ 40).

According to Federal State Statistics Service (Rosstat), the share of Russian citizens with incomes below the sub'sistence level | at the end of 2020 | decreased to 12.1% (17.8 million people) compared to 12.3% in 2019. It became possible due to additional social payments. In combination with the e'xisting targeted social assistance, these additional social payments | which are similar to universal basic income (UBI) | enabled to reduce absolute poverty.

In 2021, a decision was made on a monthly social payment in the amount of 0.5 of the regional subsistence minimum to poor single-parent families with children, as well as a similar payment to pregnant women from low-income families.

A number of additional payments were made not according to the principle of targeting, but according to the principle—to everyone. This was in line with the principle of paying an universal basic income [UBI].

An expert survey was conducted in August-October 2020 on whether Russia is ready for payments that meet the principles of an UBI. The expert group includes representatives of four categories of specialists:

- Research community (this group included 13 experts)
- Leading universities (this group included 13 experts)
- Business community and trade unions (this group consisted of 12 experts)
- State and municipal government (this group consisted of 14 experts).

We have found that experts were divided into two approximately equal groups on the issue of the possible applying of UBI in Russia. 55 percent of experts believe that Russia is ready to introduce UBI that would meet all its criteria or to transitional forms of UBI. But 45 percent of the experts believe that Russia is not ready for the introduction of UBI.

Then we worked with experts who were supported of the introduction of UBI. They answered the question about the MAIN REASONS TO INTRODUCE UBI IN RUSSIA. Several answers could be given. We have found that overwhelming majority of experts focused on the fight against poverty. 93.5 percent of the experts associate the introduction of UBI with such a goal as reducing the poverty, ensuring a "minimum standard of living for vulnerable population". Also, quite often, experts identified such goals as decreasing the socio-economic inequality (67.7%) and ensuring social justice (right to life, equal opportunities (51.6%). Labour market and employment regulation as a reason to introduce UBI in Russia turned out to be less popular among experts (38.7%).

Our research has shown that the majority of experts (more than 80%) believe that it is necessary to conduct pilot experiments on the introduction of UBI, to test its transitional forms. In our study, we also asked experts to identify the categories of the population for which they consider it appropriate to pilot the introduction of UBI. Several answers could be given. We have received the following distribution of experts preferences. The overwhelming majority of experts focused on the fight against poverty again.

We suppose it is acceptable to test some transitional forms of universal basic income in Russia (Bobkov et al., 2021; Bobkov et al., 2020a).

Firstly, for low-income families with children (a pilot project has been carried out and a simulation model has been developed)/ Low-income families with children are priority category.

Secondly, for young workers who graduated from educational institutions and entered the labour market for the first time (stages of implementation of this task has been outlined).

Thirdly, for unemployed people who were registed at employment centers (additional payments to the dole)—a simulation model has been developed).

And, finaly, for workers with risks of precarious employment, especially for workers dealing with employment based on digital platforms.

On the whole, no consensus has yet been reached in Russia on the introduction of UBI payments. Russian politicians solve the UBI problem mainly for opportunistic "purposes". There is also no consensus among Russian experts on this matter.

The application of the UBI "institute is possible only with a high degree of public consensus on following" issues (Bobkov et al., 2020b):

- about the causes of poverty and wealth;
- on the acceptable boundaries of socio-economic inequality;
- on the prospects for the ratio of working and free time;
- on the economic possibilities of introducing UBI
- and other value ideas about life in modern states.

The experience of social assistance for population in the context of the COVID-19 pandemic contributes to the solution of difficult issues related with UBI concept:

- Advantages of the unconditional principle in social support outweigh the targeted support;
- Unconditional payments do not lead to inevitable growth of inflation;
- UBI payments can be introduced without testing under crisis situations.

The above mentioned factors make it possible to use UBI payments on a larger scale in the framework of state social policy.

It is important that the combination of targeted and unconditional support measures for the poor continues in the post-COVID period, so that the amount of targeted and unconditional payments were sufficient to meet the basic needs of Russian citizens. This would make it possible to move more decisively towards overcoming absolute monetary poverty.

References

Bobkov, V. N., Kolmakov, I. B., & Odintsova, E. V. (2020). Modeling the effect of paying basic income to unemployed citizens of the Russian Federation. In *E3S Web of Conferences*, Vol. 224: Topical Problems of Agriculture, Civil and Environmental Engineering (TPACEE 2020). https://doi.org/10.1051/e3sconf/202022403004

Bobkov, V., Zolotov, A., Zolotova, M., Zolotov, S. (2020). Distribution proportional to needs as a potential element of unconditional basic income. In *CDSES. 2020 European Proceedings of Social and Behavioural Sciences EpSBS. IV International Scientific Conference "Competitiveness and the development of socio-economic systems" dedicated to the memory of Alexander Tatarkin*, pp. 1108–1114. https://doi.org/10.15405/epsbs.2021.04.116

Bobkov, V. N., Zolotov, A. V., & Odintsova, E. V. (2021). Transitional forms of unconditional basic income as a real prospect for Russia // Transition forms of universal basic income as a real prospect for Russia. *Economic and Social Changes: Facts, Trends, Forecast, 14*(4), 33–47. https://doi.org/10.15838/esc.2021.4.76.2

Solidarity as Form of Governing

Peter Herrmann

1 Introduction

Obviously, the traditional understanding of democracy is from different sides under stress. The two main aspects of the weakening of the western tradition are the following: (i) The conditions for the emergence and existence of a demos in the traditional sense do not exist anymore; (ii) at the same time the institutional system of Western democracy, fundamentally based on the western understanding of the state as representative and servant of individuals, (re-)presenting itself as quasi-individual, are dissolved in a quasi-liquid mass, not having the means of aggregating individuals' diversity nor the means of establishing and enforcing a common good or even only a common identity. In short, we can speak of an escalating and spiralling process of differentiation, by which different arrays of the economic and political are reaching a stage of near to independence. Contradictions are unavoidable consequence: this means in a negative reading that any kind of cooperation or at least coordination is becoming near to impossible; in a positive reading it can be developed in a distinctively elaborated way, reaching levels of technical perfection and being specifically targeted. While the danger of moving towards an uncontrolled undemocratic, expertocratic system cannot be denied, the possibility of an elaborated subsidiary system should also be taken into consideration. In other words, the thesis guiding the following elaboration is that we must look for new forms of governance that are suitable for an increased

P. Herrmann (✉)
Law School at the Central South University, Changsha, China
e-mail: herrmann@esosc.eu

R. D. Hepp (ed.), *Shifts and Reorientation Within the Social-Crisis and Catastrophe: Towards the Realization of Pandemic Epistemological Processes*, Prekarisierung und soziale Entkopplung – transdisziplinäre Studien,
https://doi.org/10.1007/978-3-658-43041-2_4

participation of concerned people (individuals and groups) and can serve as complement to traditional 'democratic structures' albeit the need of their reform and restructuration.

2 What is Democracy About?

Democracy is commonly understood as having a high value, apparently without any need for exploring functional aspects. It is generally seen as a value in itself, suggesting that it is a form of government that works for the people within a specified polity—for the people meaning on the one hand in their interest and on the other hand with the active involvement. The forms of involvement differ in conceptual ways, the main form being that of a representative system, established in order to allow direct involvement of those concerned, the most common being some kind of 'federalist system', with political 'parties' at their core.

However, the major challenge, democracy aims to address is not necessarily the participation of the people as value in itself; more important is maintaining the functionality and integrity of the polity in question. During earlier stages of history, the borders and subject matter of the polities have been more or less clearly defined—referring to the nation state as it emerged during the late Renaissance/ early Modernity. The understanding of these borders had been tightened by the orientation on 'gain' as described by Karl Polanyi and the subsequent establishment of the employment-related welfare state. While this is commonly understood as collective system, it is important to emphasise that the opposite is true: while we find some germs of collectivism, the overall pattern is that of an individualist system of protecting livelihood. These two features—gain-orientation and individualised welfare provision—defined substantially the nation state's core, leaving territoriality at a level of mere formality.

In detail, one may discuss some of this interpretation; but in general terms it seems to be an entirely correct view, in particular if we approach the definiendum today. In this case the focus is actually not the nation state but the functionality and integrity of a unit or different units that are independent from each other while they are by different means bound together—one of the means is purely the traditional territorial border.

While we are witnessing a partial decline of imagined communities, we see at the same time the emergence of real communities, the borders now being defined by some form of common action. In other words, we witness the emergence of spaces for action, separated from their environment by functional specification. As much as this is on the one hand a matter of disintegration it emerges at some stage as liberation from the expected subordination under extraneous rules and regulations.

3 Stages of Segregation

In the present context of contributions dealing with precarity, the following model of differentiation and segregation will be helpful to identify different stages—on the one hand sketching the sociological perspective, on the other hand qualifying the stages of segregation, reaching from integrity over functional dependency, subordination to sovereignty (the latter occurring in different forms and to different degrees).

1. Socio-Economic Integrity: Space of and for social acting, the 'economic' being an integrated and subservient part of the processes of social (re-) production.

   Production (work) being geared to immediate sustenance, the political and social being part of the sustenance production
2. Functional Dependency: Different more or less distinct systems standing by and large side by side, while gaining independence from each other. Emergence of the public, distinct from the private. Production (work) shifts with this towards being a means of 'performing in the public'. This is part of the division of labour output, namely the production of use value and exchange value.

   While the production of exchange value gains overhand, its results become means to achieve anything as far as they represent a universal form, i.e. they can be exchanged and be transformed into money
3. Subordination under Hegemonic System Requirements: One system (usually the economic, sometimes the political) gaining a dominant position, dependency not only a matter of functional dependency but of hegemony, i.e. the complete subordination as 'capital comes dripping from head to foot, from every pore, with blood and dirt of every pore' (Marx, Karl, Cap I, Ch. 31).

   Privatisation of the public including individualisation of the social; work develops its ambiguity to an extreme: being highly segmented, seemingly detached from the labour power—thus it is possible to buy/sell even tiny 'segments' (e.g. click-work). On the other hand the necessary search for niches allows looking for something that is creative, reflects personal strengths and likes

4. Sovereignty I: Gaining some independence by the subsystems, utilising system structures and reinterpreting hegemonic requirements in the light of genuinely own notions and ambitions

   As 'classical mechanisms' of making a living fail (labour, social benefits, tax breaks …), alternatives are required, normalising the anormal. Possible consequences:

   * anomy
   * revival of SME's
   * alternative market structuration, e.g. second hand business, DIY … each allowing/requiring living outside the box
5. Sovereignty II: Sovereignty in the sense of autonomous cooperative integration, cooperating along the own needs as point of departure. Shift of society/societal regulation: from employment to basic income, allowing work to be work, instead of functioning as carrier of the labour power

In short, we are dealing with a setting that is characterised by a demeaning of traditional borders, mainly referring to territory and subsequently defined national identities—the replacement/substitution follows from the fact that points that serve as reference for societal praxis shifted to other characteristics as in particular

- professional interests
- special socio-cultural identity, including sexual orientation if understood as public statement), faith
- concerns for distinct issues (environmental concerns, care for accessibility of cultural events, peace, digital communication artificial intelligence …)

While engagement in any of these areas is by no means democratically backed in a formal way, it is substantially backed by specific interests of 'concerned people'. Rules must be found, protecting processes against being dominated by economically strong interests as we are in fact on located on an interim stage—between stage 3 and 4 of the foregoing table. This is especially a challenge, as we are acting on the basis of a strong substantial interest—and a subsequent intensive engagement -and the broad concern for variety of people across the globe, while territorial borders of nation states are—at least conceptually—overcome.

4 Solidarity—A Moral Value?

In the understanding of late-capitalist or post-modern societies, solidarity seems to be redefined as matter of morality: we're talking about immoral behaviour, immoral attitudes, immoral claims and expectations, whereas it is rarely applied to structural issues. In cases serving as exception, we find even then only reference to conditions that encourage immoral behaviour and attitudes. The existential principle 'first grab, then morals' (Brecht) remains neglected, Marx' critique of 'eternal justice' ignored, stating against Proudhon who begins by taking his ideal of Justice, of 'justice éternelle', from the juridical relations that correspond to the production of commodities: thereby, it may be noted, he proves, to the consolation of all good citizens, that the production of commodities is a form of production as everlasting as justice. Then he turns round and seeks to reform the actual production of commodities, and the actual legal system corresponding thereto, in accordance with this ideal. ... Do we really know any more about 'usury', when we say it contradicts 'justice éternelle', 'équité éternelle', 'mutualité éternelle', and other 'vérités éternelles' than the fathers of the church did when they said it was incompatible with 'grâce éternelle', 'foi éternelle', and 'la volonté éternelle de Dieu'? (Marx, 1867, p. 96)

This position by Proudhon remains even behind that of outspoken classical liberals as in particular David Hume and Adam Smith. For the latter, the link between the economy and morality had been extremely close, and one may say that it had been in some respect an entity in an Aristotelean understanding of a good life, which he sees as virtue for its own sake, without being oriented towards any practical goal. There is a paradox, however: while such virtue is seen as highest value, moral sentiments are in Smith's terms by no means abstract considerations. On the contrary, it is the human practice, by way of managing reproduction and production of every day's life—and as much as these are acts, undertaken by individuals, they are still about forming a 'common standard'. This does not occur as outcome of a moral sentiment, guided by religious or similar agreements or enforcements. While approaching economic value from the standpoint of exchange, thus, of course, not as radical as Marx, Smith recognises the role the development of the productive forces. This is obvious when he refers to the cotton shirt as standard:

By necessaries I understand, not only the commodities which are indispensably necessary for the support of life, but whatever the custom of the country renders it indecent for creditable people, even of the lowest order, to be without. A linen shirt, for example, is, strictly speaking, not a necessary of life. The Greeks and Romans lived, I suppose, very comfortably, though they had no linen. But in the present times, through the greater part of Europe, a creditable day-labourer would be ashamed to appear in publick without a linen shirt, the want of which would be supposed to denote that disgraceful degree of poverty, which, it is presumed, no body can well fall into without extreme bad conduct. Custom, in the same manner, has rendered leather shoes a necessary of life in England. … (Smith, 1776, p. 869 f.)

While this paragraph is frequently referred to in order to highlight the relativity of poverty, I suggest seeing it as emphasis of the development of the productive forces, the mentioned 'extreme bad conduct' being very much a matter of low productivity rather than any form of wrong-doing by individuals. Although only through the backdoor, we see morality being (i) established (by active individuals) (ii) as objective social fact.

From here it is only a small step, undertaken by moving to the Marxist theory of value, however, considering value not as economic term in a narrow understanding but referring to the production of social value, or, in a different formulation, the value of producing also the social as value. Indeed, then the value of such production is somewhat limited, namely by the process of immediate cooperation, substantially defined by the common interest. This, then, can be seen as matter of solidarity.

Looking at the etymology of the term, highlights the following:

- firm, compact
- undivided, made from the same stuff
- well-established (Harper, 2022)

Taking this as point of departure, solidarity is already commonly taken as foundation and point of reference for acting together, for praxis of certain groups that 'belong together'. Such solidarity does not refer to a subjectively motivated 'moving together', and any 'call for solidarity' is somewhat misleading, raising awareness of commonality would be more appropriate, of course, leaving open what this commonality is and how far it can be stretched. Two main questions must be asked: (i) What kind of 'relevance' is needed for making out commonality? (ii) The second question concerns the relationality, wondering if it is necessary to speak of different solidarities, the solidarity against somebody/ a group/ class, the solidarity as immediate, perceivable consensus/commonality, solidarity as morally-perceived obligation to act, solidarity as resistance/defence?

Elaborating a tight definition along this line, we arrive at a new form of civil society—one that is not seeing itself as counterpart of the state or political lobby-group. Instead,

- it focuses on the common good A– and is in this way state-like (at least if we see the state in its own ideal self-presentation)
- it is geared to an ideal representation of neutral standards—sine ira et studio, though this Weberian statement is altered in the sense of being applied with respect of the position, while being completely denied or even reversed when looking at work and exchange in order to enhance performance
- thus it is not about competition and searching for advantage on the cost of others.

Overall, we may see it as strategy of mutual benefit in the inner structures and in the overall structure of governance at a stage where nation states loose meaning and power, while no supranational government is in sight.

5 Conclusions

Three main challenges we face are both, political and economic—and while they seem to be new, it may well be that they are only new by way of the interrelatedness and by way of their visibility (or increasing awareness and sensibility)

- the nation state and its decreasing meaning when it comes to shaping political and socio-economic processes
- the over-/supra-differentiation of society (including cutting-off of work, segmenting it into single, isolated acts]
- the partial de-meaning of productive work in the strict sense and the shift towards different kinds of services and immaterial goods.

Taken together, this results in the need for new ways of regulation and steering, searching for a balance between expert-knowledge and democratic legitimation. An African saying suggests 'If you want to go fast, go alone; if you want to go far, go together.' The question remains that of defining the goal in substantial terms—such determination is itself concerned with this dilemma of speed and depth. The entire problematique is only becoming virulent under conditions of far-reaching change—in other words under the condition of crisis, which according to Antonio Gramsci 'the crisis consists precisely in the fact that the old is dying and the new cannot be born; in that interim period a great variety of morbid symptoms appear.' (Gramsci, António, 1930: Quaderni del carcere, vol. I: quaderni 1.5; Edizone Critica del Istituto Gramsci a Cura di Valentino Gerratana;

Torino: Giulio Einaudi, 1975, p. 311 xyz; translation P.H.) Morbid symptoms is here understood in a very wide sense, also containing possible elements of a positive drive, contributing to overcoming the illness of the old system. Suggesting that solidarity may serve as means of introducing a bit of the veil which enforces decisions that consider the worse-off situation. One of the main reasonings behind the argument is that members of the precariat are not just experts in assessing precarity; at least they are also experts in the said alternatives or in working under conditions that may be considered as the new normal, for the time being in one or another way still behind the veil of ignorance (Rawls). It is not just about flexibility come on adaptability come on security and the lack of it; in this light it is also about the search for new solidarity shaping a global social economic power balance. Alluding to the famous passage from Goethe's (1808) Faust Statutes and laws that we inherit, /Like an eternal malady,/Go trailing on from race to race,/And furtive shift from place to place./To nonsense reason turns,/and benefit to worry./Woe unto you that you're a grandchild, woe!/For of the law that was born with us, no!/ Of that, alas! there never is a query (translated by George Madison Priest; https://web.archive.org/web/20130331154558/ http://www.einam.com/faust/index.html; 13/07/2020 xyz) we may suggest that realism is nonsense, and functioning should make us worry; needed is utopia, a new understanding of security and new ways of thinking about its beneficiaries—radically!

References

von Goethe, J. W. (1808). *Faust. Eine Tragoedie.* Cotta, S. 121. http://www.deutschestextarchiv.de/book/view/goethe_faust01_1808?p=127. Accessed July 13, 2020. Translated by George Madison Priest; https://web.archive.org/web/20130331154558/ http://www.einam.com/faust/index.html. Accessed July 13, 2020.

Gramsci, A. (1930). *Quaderni del carcere. In Quaderni 1.5; Edizone Critica del Istituto Gramsci a Cura di Valentino Gerratana* (Vol. I). Giulio Einaudi.

Harper, D. (2022). *Etymology of solidarity.* Online Etymology Dictionary. https://www.etymonline.com/word/solidarity. Accessed September 23, 2022.

Marx, K. (1867). Capital, volume one. In K. Marx & F. Engels (Hrsg.), *Collected works* (Vol. 35). Lawrence & Wishart.

Smith, A. (1776). *An inquiry into the nature and causes of the wealth of nations.* In R. H. Campbell, A. S. Skinner, W. B. Todd (Hrsg.) (Vol. II). Liberty Press (Reprint. Originally published: Clarendon Press, 1979, Glasgow edition of the works and correspondence of Adam Smith; 2, 1976)

Education Systems, Lockdown, and Restrictions: Education Reconsidered

Fernando Marhuenda-Fluixá

This contribution is a personal, yet professional reflection based upon an overview of several international and Spanish national reports on the impact of the Corona-pandemic upon education systems (compulsory level and upper secondary education, adult education, special education; but I do not include here reference nor reflection regarding university studies) as well as non-formal education in different shapes (from social education to leisure education).

I look back to the ongoing education processes under lockdown in the first half of 2020 and the reopening of schools in some countries in the second half of 2020, while there have been countries where reopening has taken two years. The extent to which the way governments, families, teachers and students have handled education will help us consider to what extent education, particularly basic and compulsory level, is an activity that can be referred to as an essential service.

I also deal with the effect of delivering child and youth education in hybrid ways, hence questioning the face-to-face relation that was considered as a given fact at the center of the education practice, even in debates in the past decades on homeschooling. By doing so, I will address organizational, curricular and assessment facets of education under pandemics, and I question what is understood by education practice given the restrictions and conditions that have allowed it to

F. Marhuenda-Fluixá (✉)
University of Valencia, Valencia, Spain
e-mail: Fernando.Marhuenda@uv.es

R. D. Hepp (ed.), *Shifts and Reorientation Within the Social-Crisis and Catastrophe: Towards the Realization of Pandemic Epistemological Processes*, Prekarisierung und soziale Entkopplung – transdisziplinäre Studien,
https://doi.org/10.1007/978-3-658-43041-2_5

continue. I will conclude my reflection with a balance between the evident and the groundswell transformations that education may be going through, and which are the challenges ahead.

1 Introduction

The writer of this paper works in university (higher education), my research focuses upon vocational education and training (the education of young adults, at the post-compulsory level) and upon early school leaving; and the Coronavirus and the lockdown following the pandemic meant leaving school and changed forms of attendance). Priorities in education changed, though some resisted to change, and the inertias of the school system were and are very strong.

Educational practice has to do with personal trust and social bonds. Education in nation states in the past two centuries has been shaped as a presential system, as a system of mass education, including physical attendance for teaching and learning but also for control purposes—and control survived to the lockdown and restrictions that followed.

Educational practice happens in many sites of life, but it is schools which have the monopoly over the right to basic education. Educational practice in schools is shaped by routine, and it is routine that provides and guarantees stability of education systems. Education was a responsibility assumed in the nineteenth century by the Nation State which took it over from families, not without discussion over whose responsibility it is to educate the next generation and why should public authorities interfere within the private domain of families. During lockdown this responsibility was temporarily devolved to families and their assistance in keeping the system online was necessary.

There is a conflict inherent to school education, between content delivery and relational activity, between transmission of knowledge and personal and social development. During lockdown, content won preeminence and relations lost relevance, banks of content resources were offered as a solution to the situation. Disciplines were more relevant than the hidden curriculum, which did not vanish but did not change either, it was only reinforced by social inequalities related to family socioeconomic living conditions. The online expansion of schooling did not satisfy the purposes of comprehensive education, and content rather than competencies spread across all curricular areas, as content can be easily delivered online, far more than competencies.

Despite schooling being a public measure, private school funding has become common in many countries, as another way of families counteracting the weight of the State in decisions upon the education of their children and youth. During the Coronavirus crisis, public and private schools took decisions upon very different material conditions; different reactions to the customer were adopted by privately funded schools, whether it was directly paid (a service to be consumed should be offered) or not, relying upon many different electronic tools and applications that had been a minor part of schooling until then. This happened in all countries, though in some it had very detailed constrains, like Uganda, where access to data or even electricity was and has been key in guaranteeing access to education. The very notion of access to education has been replaced by accessing distance learning resources, even if these are not the same.

Until the pandemic, education was face-to-face, real; during lockdown it turned virtual, and it has recovered its presential shape even if masked. The trend seems, however, that school education will return to the old normal as soon as possible, so strong is its inertia. Education was managed by the Nation State as a social relation; nevertheless during lockdown it turned into an individual activity (but not an individualized one, often rather standardized). Among the different meanings of education (*Bildung*, citizenship, economic progress, acculturation, socialization, and personal development among others), during the Coronavirus crisis some took over the others and it became clear what was considered most valuable of education, what had to remain even if it was confined: Content. This may have caused damage ignoring other dimensions of both education and schooling. School routines tend to be rigid, Covid demanded flexibilization, and the school has shown its capacity to be flexible in ways of handling the curriculum as well as in finding ways for applying assessment criteria during lockdown. When back to normal, school has been quick to recover its traditional ways, and year 2023 witnessed how countries and families are rejecting the use of screens and virtual platforms in schools.

What happened in schools might have happened differently: From a sabbatical for all, both teachers and students, to give more appreciation to the worth of non-formal learning, without this implying a rupture with the school system. When education recovered, it took the shape of masked teaching. Whether distanced and masked are attributes that can match educational activity (that in early stages like child or primary education has always required closeness and face-to-face, to personalize the relation and satisfy the individual educational needs and avoid anonymization), is one more of the contradictions of school, often tending to standardize.

2 Coronavirus, a Global Crisis

The Coronavirus spread since late 2019 and in accelerated and global ways since March 2020 all throughout the world: The pandemic has been a prototype for what a global crisis may be look like, one that is not restricted to geographical areas, social classes, different economies … Indeed, it has had global resonance, although that could also be said about climate change and climate crisis (despite the effects of these manifest themselves differently according to world regions), while the Coronavirus had a similar effect all over the world.

Its impact upon education has been great and sudden, though perhaps more short-term that one might expect; while its impact upon learners, children and young people, has been both short and long-term. Its impact upon well-established education systems in affluent countries may have seemed new despite there are populations in those countries that have often suffered discrimination, but there are other situations in recent decades where education systems of different countries have seen their work interrupted and in abrupt ways.

Some examples of these may be traced in education systems of countries with little international acknowledgement and suffering war within their borders, such as Palestine or the Sahara, that are used to such interruptions as well as to postponing the opening of schools, sometimes subject to physical reasons as clear as bombing of the buildings. More recently, that has also been the case in the Ukraine, at the heart of Europe itself, due to the Russian invasion in February 2022. No surprise that the lessons learned and the technological solutions developed during the Coronavirus have proved useful to adapt that education system to conditions of functioning under an ongoing war, at least in the Ukrainian ruled schools: certainly, those schools which are now ruled by Russia will continue their work though under new regulations, probably having an effect upon the curricula as well as teaching staff. If education is often subject to the ideological and cultural struggles within a certain society, these will only reinforce when there is an open war (among others, upon language, history and geographical borders, what we could summon under the humanities area of the curriculum).

There are other examples we may refer to: education in developing countries, whose education systems have not yet reached features known to Western Europe such as mass education or universalization to both children and young people. There are parts in the world where education is only provided privately because the government has not the capacity (or the will) to manage it, while in other regions the material conditions of living attract and recruit children to work, sometimes under conditions of slavery, even if they are at an age where they should be attending school. There are also parts of the world where it is particularly girls who are neglected the chance to continue their schooling, specifically when they grow as young women and can therefore reproduce. These cases are particularly painful and yet school attendance is interrupted at a too early age—without a virus provoking it, and repeatedly, year after year.

Another example we could refer to is that of young people enrolled in schools in refugee camps all over the world; people that have been forced to flee their homes and to leave their schools behind, that gather in settlements which are conceived as provisory although too often they become permanent, and which grow to the size of large urban cities with regulations of their own, also sharing a particular form of lockdown: movement is restricted to the space within the borders of the refugee camp.

My introductory point is, therefore, that the effects of lockdown in schools due to Coronavirus in 2020 were new for many but part of the ordinary way to deal with everyday school life for many others in the world too. This is something to take into consideration to relativize arguments used in many Western countries about the difficulties and even impossibilities brought by the virus. The right to education, the right to basic education, with its reverse side in compulsory attendance to school, cannot be taken for granted in the third decade of the twenty-first century, even if it may seem so to many of us.

3 Covid-19 and Education

Although this paper is on education, those involved in the school system (students, families, teachers, counselors, social educators, managers, administrators, side services, companies in the case of vocational education and training) were subject to other crises: First and mainly, health, both physical and mental, as the fears about the unknown were very present from the very beginning of the crisis and they led to isolation in many different forms. Second, an economic crisis, provoked by the lockdown and the interruption of many economic activities, those considered non-essential, or their move towards online activities where possible, like the case of education. Third, a world crisis: there was nowhere to scape, the whole globe was affected and the reaction seemed to be for everyone to go back home, which implies a home of one's own with conditions that allow life under lockdown, but also entries of food and beverages among others, so that life can proceed and not be interrupted. Fourth, a systemic crisis, one having an impact upon all social classes, all sectors of society, all countries despite their size and wealth. A crisis that manifested itself very clearly in the health systems, pushed to their limits; in the pharmaceutical industry, cooperating while competing in order to get effective and efficient vaccination; in the countries' economies; in the sector of transport and logistic, which was significantly reduced and resulted in the lowest levels of pollution known in decades; in tourism, that was cancelled; but also manifested in minor yet relevant everyday details such as the impossibility to say goodbye to the relatives that were dying (with disregard whether due to the Coronavirus or to all other illnesses that did not interrupt); and in many other domains of ordinary life.

But it is an educational crisis that we are considering here. However, maybe we have to elucidate first whether it is educational or rather academic, or which of both is more relevant. The crisis is educational insofar it affects both formal and non-formal education. It is not just educational levels that are affected, from child education to preparation of access to university; from ordinary schooling to schooling serving people with special education needs; from the education of children and youth to adults enrolled in adult education programs; as well as for different forms and levels of vocational education, training and qualification in school-based systems as well as in dual systems, these ones strongly affected in those sectors of activity interrupted during the lockdown. Second chance schools, as well as many different kinds of training provision for early school leavers was also affected, even if often out of sight, scope and regulation from the education system authorities.

It was not only education as curriculum delivery that was affected by the crisis: all extracurricular activities related to the school were also interrupted or altered (private companies offering such services sought alternative ways to provide their services and get their income as well), as well as side services such as early hours or school canteens and school transport.

Let us remind about other forms of education, non-formal and formal, that is provided in particular regulated conditions, such as the education of people in prisons (already education in lockdown before the lockdown was even decreed) or the education of children and youth in shelter homes through the social protection system: this latter one had to continue, but lockdown was felt here very differently, as it suffered all of the constrains with little room to find freedom of spirit and body other than that provided by the educators in those institutions who were, at the same time, suffering the impact of the virus on the rest of dimensions of their lives. Similar comments may be made upon day care centers of children and young people, of institutions offering education and occupational training and therapy to people with disabilities, institutions in-between education and work like special employment centers or all the educational services provided by non-for profit organizations that have a say upon the education of citizens all around the world.

Furthermore, most activities related to leisure education were also cancelled, postponed, or severely altered, and the institutions behind them had to look for alternative ways to conduct their businesses, when that was the case, or how to reconduct their activities when it comes to voluntary work, such as the kind offered in organizations known worldwide like the scout movement.

There is also a whole array of institutions that, despite not having an educational mission, develop educational activities to spread their aims, and they often seek to do so around or within the education system. Such educational approaches include those such as the promotion of diversity of different kinds, approaches towards a global citizenship, peace education, environmental education, anti-racist education, or more specific matters such as sexual education or sports. Most of these are often provided by NGOs and civic organizations who take the advantage of compulsory school as an appropriate audience to deliver their message, and most of their messages are often welcome by teachers in schools.

One lesson I expect to have made clear is that education is much more than schooling, much more than formal education, even though most of the reports that have been produced about the impact of the Coronavirus upon education are limited to the education systems and to the academic services they provide to children and youth.

Another lesson, however, refers to the perception of the crisis among different actors within the education system: the viewpoints of teachers, students, families, the administration, or employers do not necessarily coincide, while these discourses are also heterogeneous within each of those groups, not only for ideological reasons but also with the everyday experience of the crisis. All of these, of course, without forgetting that if there were homogeneous views these would only be appropriate for a certain level of the education system but not the others, for the different aims, expectations and demands that shape their structuring.

A final lesson is about the weight of other crises. Let me remember that it was only in December 2019 that the Global Climate Summit took place in Madrid (after Chile declined), with Greta Thunberg as an acknowledged voice to claim urgent action to address global warming and climate change; a crisis that seems to have been swept away by the virus.

4 Education Under Lockdown

The Coronavirus spread and in March 2020 many countries adopted measures affecting daily life in all domains, also affecting education provision. The most severe decision was to approve temporary lockdowns, indicating the need to avoid as many activities out of home as possible. Education, an activity that for centuries humankind developed at home, had been outsourced to the education systems only in the past two centuries, and mass universal education had been achieved in many countries only after World War II. Homeschooling was a minority practice, sometimes promoted by communities of anarchist ideology who resisted the State intervention in any domain of life for taking away individual responsibility and freedom, and in recent decades demanded by conservative families very eager to decide upon what must be taught to their children and youth and who mistrust the State claiming an ideological bias that they do not recognize in themselves. Who holds the right to education is mistaken in these debates for whom is accountable of education. Anyhow, if the trend in the past two centuries in Western societies had been towards education system taking over the role of families in providing (school) education to their children; national lockdown including education implied the devolution of education to happen at home, even if still expected to be delivered by teachers, professionals is another way to put it, instead of amateurs.

This is therefore the first consequence of lockdown: education returned to the home space, but not withholding the intrusion of teachers in decisions about content, method, and assessment.

Before going into further detail on what this may imply, it is worth considering the conditions in which school education at home had to take place.

The first of these conditions tackles what was lacking: the absences that were remarkable in addressing a new way to teach. Lack of time was undoubtedly the first and most relevant aspect and, indeed a surprise, it seems that lack of time and therefore of planning was not a problem to keep educating in a remote system or, in other ways, not to interrupt the role of school. Of course, the continuation of education, even if online, was a necessary contribution to allow the implementation of home-office in all occupational sectors that were allowed to do so, as the function of custody of school was more clearly marked than ever before in the last hundred years. Lack of time comes together with lack of intention or direction, lack of knowledge, lack of decisions emanating from the authorities too. Education should go on and no-one doubted that it could be able to proceed on a distance basis. No alternative was considered, not in the first moments, while other professional sectors discussed how to continue with their activity. For education, online was the only choice and an appropriate one.

However, teachers all over the world are trained to teach face-to-face, and distance learning had been used rather as continuous training for staff development and adult education, also in higher education, but not that much in compulsory education (even though there were experiences with radio education in the 1970s in different parts of Australia, for instance). If we think of school, the image that comes to our minds is that of a classroom packed with students: the classroom was missing during lockdown. Adequate training to conduct online education was also missing: the most urgent decision was not a pedagogical but a technological one, which online platform to use among the several available, some free of charge (in exchange of sharing your data) and some subject to market license. Once the platform was chosen, the next step was to provide basic information to teachers on how to make use of the basic functions of the platform and, from then on, to let the teacher explore further possibilities. Any pedagogical concern of the effects of using the platforms, on the adaptation of teachers' styles, methods, approach to teaching and to the subject, on how well these fit the technical requirements of the platforms was ignored. It was urgent to keep instruction, and the urgency to continue was more relevant than the effects of continuation under very different conditions of delivery.

Lack of time and lack of training were accompanied by lack of resources. The availability of resources for homeschooling was not provided by the school system, it was the responsibility of families to get the necessary equipment to facilitate connection on online classes, from the devices (smartphones, computers, laptops, tablets) to the service provider (the telephone company). Here, of course, we come to a new dimension of inequalities in education, where traditional impact of economic possibilities on education chances (a room of one's own to study, a place to study, a library at home; not to mention enrolment in extracurricular, support and supplementary activities) was suddenly confronted with a new situation: having to share the same equipment with your siblings or even parents, who needed to use it simultaneously, not just to attend the classes but also to do the homework and assignments: all classroom activity had suddenly become homework. Of course, there were individual teachers and individual families who took the effort to guarantee sufficient supply of these equipment and connections, but the system failed to give an answer to a problem that the system had caused itself by moving towards distance learning.

There was also lack of clear guidelines: the decision to interrupt face-to-face schooling was so dramatic that any alternative, no matter which technological support it might receive, proved inappropriate and, therefore, authorities responsible to take decisions in both democratic and authoritarian school systems were reluctant to do so, and they often yielded great amount of autonomy to individual schools and teachers, conscious that they were not able to provide the material conditions necessary to implement distance learning. By doing so, authorities failed teachers and schools at a moment when governance, shared governance but with a clear direction, was certainly needed. That lack of guidelines resulted in a vast array of decisions and practice that, once again, caused an increase in inequalities within the education system which is paradoxically believed to play a major role in reducing and tackling those inequalities.

The lack of time, training, resources, and guidance was not, however, an issue strong enough to reconsider whether school should continue face-to-face instead of online and whether, in the case of online, education practice could be temporarily withheld so that teachers were trained and prepared to address distance education in proper conditions. Interruption was not a choice, for the custody function mentioned above, and continuity was therefore assumed.

The lesson I want to extract here is that considering the lack of appropriate conditions one might have assessed the possibility to interrupt schooling or to continue with it altering the conditions for face-to-face teaching, the same way that many other activities continued face-to-face with health and safety measures that proved effective enough.

Continuation of education was taken for granted, and it was so under the assumption that school could resume in the very same place where it had left it before the lockdown. Continuation was possible because of the will to do so by teachers, because of their professional responsibility. However, we must be aware that voluntary work and education system do not match together properly, as the provision of compulsory education, of formal education, is a highly regulated activity, subject to decisions on curriculum (allocation of time and content), pedagogy (a method to deliver content that is conditioned by organizational decisions such as grouping, time schedules, teaching or co-teaching) and particularly of assessment, an assessment that leads to official qualifications and grades. The fact that voluntary work is performed by the professionals hired by the system cannot be left aside either.

Schooling continued out of schools and got itself embedded into every home, it was not interrupted, not even to decide on the best way to proceed even if interruption in schooling is however a frequent act: schooling stops every weekend, every festivity, be it national or local, there are holiday periods without classes … but the Coronavirus could not result in interrupting schooling. Voluntarism of teachers guaranteed such a continuation, despite lacking time, preparation, resources, and planning; all of which led to great disparity.

Continuation happened in very different ways among each individual school in the same town or region, among levels of education in which students of the same families were enrolled, among family possibilities of students enrolled in the same schools; and certainly, among different school systems all throughout the world according to their resources and governance.

When lockdown was decreed, the reaction of school systems was to continue in on-line mode, with the assumed aim to provide a minimum of education. There was no prior estimation of the consequences of doing so and of reacting in different alternative ways: interrupting, postponing, respecting face-to-face teaching, altering the organization of presential schooling to guarantee school attendance while minimizing the risk of infection.

There has hardly been any evaluation of the result of such measure, whether it brought gains or losses to the population, whether continuing education online was better than non-continuing it or by having focused upon the most vulnerable students (in terms of learning, which often means in terms of socioeconomic circumstances: those who most needed school). There has been no evaluation of the effects of such continuation on the inequalities in education. There has been some recent literature on the consequences of online education upon learning in different facets: academic performance is the main variable analyzed, but there are others that have not been tackled yet, such as the motivation of students towards learning, towards learning online and towards moving back to learning in schools once the lockdown was over. Neither has it been addressed how habits of learning and studying and performing academic and learning tasks have changed due to online teaching; nor about the overload of tasks and the overlap of demands set by different subjects, particularly in low and upper secondary education. No study has been released so far on the impact of online teaching upon relations: personal relations in schools, relations with students, peer relations in the classroom or relations to families.

Something that continuation facilitated, nevertheless, was the opportunity for schools and their members to avoid entering the shock that the pandemics might have caused. Continuation seemed to provide certain sense of normality to the school, even though school routines were altered and substituted by new classroom routines. The school as a unit disappeared as such behind the screen. Education sorted out the lockdown and survived it.

5 Education Restricted

Once the lockdown was over, and as the different waves of the Coronavirus hit different regions and countries, considering also that schoolyears vary across hemispheres and different geographical regions, school started reopening. Some did so before the end of the schoolyear, while other school systems could only reopen in the new schoolyear, and some took even longer and have only recently reopened. In those cases that reopened early, such as Spain and other European countries, there were plans to go back to face-to-face teaching in secure environments in terms of Coronavirus infection, these plans often protocolized and adapted for the circumstances of individual schools, according to climate conditions, size, staff, and material resources available among others. These plans had to consider the possibility to introduce a new lockdown of the school, and how this would happen if it were needed. Furthermore, such plans also considered the combination of face-to-face with online and distance teaching, not only for the event of a new lockdown, but to facilitate attendance of both students and teachers that might be infected and yet feel sufficiently well enough to maintain attendance and accomplishment of home and classwork.

The implications of such combinations and the possibility to have teachers or students attending from home instead as in face-to-face were not properly considered: how would families achieve and guarantee that.

School Protocols on Health and Safety

In some cases, schools were used as an appropriate place to identify and diagnose the expansion and decrease of the different waves, as well as the impact of people gatherings in holidays and festivities upon infection at mass scale. This was so considered once it was assumed that infection among children was fast but not as dangerous as among adult population.

Safety and health procedures for the virus were implemented, affecting pedagogical measures such as grouping of students or conditions of teaching (use of mask to address students, letting noise from outside interfere with the teaching as windows were open), as well as other health measures (teaching in open spaces and keeping classrooms highly ventilated even in the middle of the coldest winter days). The interaction of students among them, within and between groups as well as with their teachers was ruled through these procedures, and it implied a significant alteration of ordinary social interactions in everyday life in schools.

There was more emphasis put in the design and implementation of procedures than in the investment in infrastructure that might improve the conditions of such procedures, including staff and support aids as well as reductions of ratios, though these happened in some school systems. There was also emphasis on training to prepare and follow the protocols (as well as to conduct registries of the infection to report to the health authorities) instead of developing appropriate training to perform pedagogically in harsh teaching conditions, with restrictions upon contact and social relations, nor on effective combination of face-to-face and online teaching.

One thing seems clear, nevertheless: when schools reopened, the aim was to go back to the previous normal as soon as possible, there was no attempt to adopt any of the measures that the transformation of schooling through Coronavirus had brought. School systems stuck up to their usual ways, there was a neglect of change.

The Roles of Schooling

If during the lockdown educational practice had suffered of altered relations and social links, having lost the relevance of eye contact and face-to-face relation; if teachers had lost control of the class and of the group because of the non-physical presence of students; if new ways to socialize (among students, with families, among colleagues and teacher-student relations) had developed, when schools reopened these were hindered and replaced by the old traditional ways of conducting such relations.

Socialization has to do with pedagogical and organizational arrangements, such as grouping of students, which is often combined with individual tasks and decisions on timing and pacing of activities. But socialization is also strongly rooted in many other side-facets of everyday life in schools: extracurricular activities, ordinary activities such as breaks, lunch, early entry activities, leisure and sports related to the school like and its relation to other schools with which there is cooperation and sports competition.

Socialization is however one more function of the system, which plays several roles in society: transmission of knowledge, which is not only teaching but also transmission and reproduction of culture and the provision of a national identity; accreditation and certification of knowledge acquisition, which is very relevant and one that has been affected (the discussion upon lowering levels of demand, that I address below). Custody, which was a clear role in former decades has now recovered weight, as the lockdown made it visible how hard it is for modern families to combine and reconcile working times with paying attention to the children. When reopening the system, custody has increased its weight as a function that the system must pay nowadays, and this is perhaps the explanation behind not considering interruption of schooling as an alternative during lockdown.

Something that became clear when schools reopened was the emotional impact of the lockdown and the effect it was having upon personal development. Schools tend to see this as a problem affecting learning and social relations, as well as perhaps a new responsibility that society is going to demand of them. But chances of schools to address this problem are scarce, and they have accomplished the aim to identify it and bring it to the public debate.

Curriculum

In the case of curriculum, both lockdown and reopening contributed to strengthen the importance of basic education and minimum content, resulting in guaranteeing access of all to education but lowering expectations to a minimum. Debates on 'back to basics' held in the past two decades have been sorted out by the pandemic in a matter of months.

Furthermore, moving to distance learning and adapting to hybrid sources of information has questioned the role of teachers in handling information, but also brings in debates about the relevance of knowledge and competence, what is expected from students in terms of learning outcomes. Disciplinary barriers may have reinforced during these past two years, as the results of the back-to-basics approach and the efforts to keep education safe within the limits of each of the subjects. This has also to do with the competence of teachers and the safety they feel around their own disciplinary background, hence upgrading the worth of academic content in opposition to practical education–practice had to be reconsidered in search of the rigidities imposed by health and safety plans, that difficulted flexibility measures aimed at attending the diversity of learners in the class. Standardization of the minimum curriculum has advanced with education under restriction conditions.

Assessment

We have reviewed different functions of the system, certification being one of them. Certification depends upon assessment procedures. Assessment and the results it showed, both at the individual as well as at the school level, soon became the most important issue for the educational administration. Once assumed that education might continue online but without proper pedagogical conditions, once assumed that decisions allowed for survival of the schoolyear, not much more could be expected and the major concerns turned towards assessment and recognition of learning. Once assumed that the curriculum delivered would only aim at basic minimum requirements, how to translate that into assessment practice? Furthermore, once assumed that the material conditions of learning of students would differ substantially and some would not be able to reconnect, for they had major needs: could assessment be used to document such inequalities?

Assessment of learning consists in the measurement of performance of students in different subjects under equal conditions, and those conditions were now different, particularly during lockdown, as they were provided at home, but also after reopening, as it was soon discovered that the effect of the lockdown upon learning processes and personal and social development had been great.

Even if assessment is used to qualify and classify, it cannot be used exactly as such if the conditions of learning are not standardized—and conditions of learning varied extremely once schools reopened, according to their material and socioeconomic conditions of their surroundings.

Therefore, assessment has been altered during these past two years, even though there are struggles to keep it useful and equal to fulfil its functions without causing major damage to those who learn worse, slower or under limited conditions. However, assessment has a public relevance, and its value has public acknowledgement. Therefore, assessment was debated, then facilitated and made-up so that the impact of the pandemic upon learning would not increase by showing it also in terms of public results.

Governance

One may conclude that assessment is in fact more relevant than curriculum or teaching, as debates over how assessment would be addressed in lockdown, and what would it imply in terms of retention and progression for the reopening of schools were the most relevant debates in 2020. These decisions were taken to avoid trouble with families and teachers, to reduce the pressure put upon them, with certain disregard for the quality of education practice and learning processes. In the reopening of schools, autonomy of decisions was provided to adapt health and safety protocols, but such an autonomy did not reach other decision areas such as curriculum arrangements or pedagogical practice.

If all decisions during lockdown and the reopening of the system were hard and controversial, participation might have contributed to ease them. Nevertheless, it was difficult to address participation in difficult circumstances for everybody and with all areas of ordinary life altered by the ways humankind was addressing this crisis. The will of going back to normal could not be addressed without investment and public policies, but there were also attempts to take advantage of the situation and search for a new normal life, a claim that had been raised already during the 2008 Great Financial Crisis. Before this disjunctive, managerial approaches were preferred to addressing decisions in pedagogical directions. The past, the known, the former normal was felt as secure and safe, a place to return rather than exploring new ways. Yet, reopening of schools was showing that the old normal was not at reach, not for the schoolyear 21/22.

Finally, it is worth noting that the reopening of schools has come together with a reinforcement of the schools' isolation from its nearest environment. Reopening of schools aimed to let students enter them, while trying to keep other agents out of their walls and restricting the cooperation that once characterized the role schools play in their local communities in different parts of the world. When reopening, making schools safe for children and youth implied to keep other people out of them, a decision reversing the trend that had marked schools all over the globe in the past decades.

6 Is the System Nude?

The past three schoolyears have been affected by the pandemic: from the lockdown to the reopening under restricted conditions, and then to reopening under masked use, have altered the meaning of face-to-face teaching. How have these affected the system? Can schools remain as if nothing had happened? Are schools able to plan changes, now that change has been made possible by a tiny virus and all of a sudden, with no prior announcement, with no strategic planning?

What Proves Obvious

Teaching and learning were a face-to-face practice that required to be present, and that was intrinsic to the way schools worked. Online learning has altered that assumption, and distance learning is now a possibility not only for higher or continuing education, but also for child, primary and secondary education, for compulsory education. Distance learning can get rid of the constrains of time and space and claims to be able to address individual needs and satisfy different pace and content delivery, though it brings along other problems. If face-to-face teaching is not needed, why should attendance to school remain compulsory? Schedules are devised around subjects and structure teachers work, but they are designed for group standardized teaching.

Family-school relations have also changed with this crisis. Two centuries of the state taking over the role of families in educating the next generations have been questioned by several months of lockdown and restricted education where school demanded the support of families in new ways. Meanwhile families have also renewed their awareness of the role of custody of schools but also of the limitations of their work.

Two issues have come to the forefront as the most relevant in terms of learning and progress of students, and those have been assessment of learning, with the side-effect of qualifying, classifying and differentiating; and transitions along schoolyears and between levels, related to the choices and restrictions of students in their progress along the different levels and chances that each school system offers them. Both assessment and transition can be addressed from the perspective of the individuals, though debates have arisen at the social level, stressing the importance of schooling in classifying and segregating people according to academic performance rather than to the education or personal and social development that they show. At a time when competences seem to have more weight than knowledge or information on the different subjects, it is academic subjects what holds the key when it comes to assessment and progress.

At the same time, school systems under the pandemic have also revealed some of their weaknesses. First, pastoral care fell low among the main worries during the lockdown and, however, it might have played a very relevant role, if academic subjects would have yielded some of their weight. This is indeed related to the emotional but also the socio-educational support that is provided in schools, and that is often provided by assistant staff. The Coronavirus crisis have devolved more weight to the subject teachers and has hindered other non-teaching roles that have become relatively common in the past three decades (careers, pastoral care, social work), roles whose incorporation to school is still fragile but which might have contributed to deal better with the personal, emotional, and social needs of so many students and their families during these troubled times.

These are roles that perhaps need more face-to-face intervention and that cannot be delivered as easily through distance learning, because there is a need to find trust and confidence in a relation that becomes more personal and that fosters not only personal development and wellbeing but also socialization of individuals in the communities they belong to.

What Remains Hidden

Beyond those rather evident dimensions that I have just commented, perhaps so evident that they are sometimes transparent and not so easy to be seen at first sight, there are other dimensions of life in schools and educational practice the Coronavirus crisis have brought to the front.

First, the measurement of time and the pace of timing in education. The Coronavirus appearance and the lockdown, decreed temporarily and prolonged as the crisis evolved, have shown that education can be paced in different ways, that there is no need to rush but perhaps it is more relevant to address learning processes with calm; that wasting time can be a way to improve learning processes. This implies a profound alteration of the industrial structure of schooling but also of current ways to look at societal processes, where speed is valued as a relevant asset. This crisis and its impact upon education remind us that education progress and success is often a matter of patience and something that can be fostered and assessed in the long run, rather than a series of speed races that happen term after term, schoolyear after schoolyear. If we take this claim seriously, if the long-term regains value in education, not only learning but also assessment will probably change and improve—to the better.

Another aspect of education that the crisis has brought to the surface is that of the limits of education: what can be expected of education, which are the functions it can fulfil, and which are the responsibilities that it cannot accountable for, what are the different roles and which cooperation may be provided among schools and families. It has also shown that teaching–learning relations are not causal but of probabilistic nature, that learning is supported or hindered by teaching but they are different processes; and that teaching is still nowadays needed to a large extent in order to structure and pace the process of learning, to bring certain equilibrium and to facilitate the next generations access to the common basic curriculum that the community and society they belong to have agreed as the minimum necessary knowledge.

Of course, this opens a very relevant question on whether schooling needs to be compulsory and, if the answer is a positive one, why is it that it has not been considered in these past years as an essential activity, one that should keep running face-to-face, as many other services. The fact that school education switched to distance education instead of looking for alternatives (i. e., letting the most vulnerable students and those without equipment attend schools, were they could receive education but also lunch, hygiene, and care; or arranging schooling in similar ways to the health system, establishing times for teachers to share with students either individually or in small groups; or extending school times to facilitate attendance of all along the different hours of the day; and others) made it a non-essential activity, one that is not necessary for survival, one that may be disposable, postponed or offered online. Online is fine for adult population when we are conscious about our responsibilities and duties; but it is probably not the best chance for people who are growing up and who must learn to certain standards that they cannot determine by themselves.

These, together with the fact that it is the academic content which has regained weight in the education process, the subjects, those that are assessed, that it is the curriculum what counts; brings to the forefront another relevant question: who is the educated person? Are we educated according to the amount of knowledge accumulated, and where do other dimensions of the person fit, some of them cognitive but others emotional and social? This is indeed an issue which refers and questions directly the goals of education, and something that makes us think why the pandemic has been ignored as a curricular content itself while it was having such a huge impact upon the life of all of us in society, and something that we will probably have to address in the coming years, as we start to address the personal, social and emotional effects of the pandemic upon people's development and relations.

7 Education Post-Covid. Advancing Education?

More than two years after the pandemic was declared as such by the World Health Organization, it seems that education systems all over the world have been able to reopen and go back to the previous ordinary way of functioning. Perhaps in a few months there will be no trace of the effect of the virus upon schools, other than the gap in learning quantity and quality that these years may have left, nothing that education systems cannot cope with. It may be therefore a good moment to consider how these could transform education, what could be generated anew, and which dimensions could education systems drop.

The pandemic has showed chances to transform several aspects of education. The first of them, mass education, given that lockdown and restricted education have demanded greater efforts to individualize education. Criteria on how to group students and decisions to introduce support teachers in the classroom have been tried these three years and some might remain and contribute to make mass education less massive. Compulsory education is not at risk, but graduated school might suffer changes because of the pressures that schools have suffered these years.

Guidance services have also to adapt to new circumstances, as it is not so evident now that decisions on careers will remain the same. Together with changes in the workplace and in work relations, the impact of the Coronavirus crisis upon certain occupational areas is worth considering by guidance staff, as students' expectations may vary as well. A notion coined in 2019, the great resignation or Big Quit, related to the job expectations of the Generation Z, may be even greater after the pandemic, as people have discovered the relevance of other areas of life than just work. In this regard, what people expect from education, from compulsory education, from vocational education too, may demand alternative educational offerings from the system.

Inclusive education has been also greatly affected by the Coronavirus, and it demands more adaptation from the system, which is also required in terms to overcome the increase in inequalities of access and achievement that these past schoolyears have showed.

These years have also indicated ways to create new chances in the provision of education in school systems. There is an increasing claim to consider personal development and personal needs in education, other than academic curriculum. Care and mental health have also gained terrain in the common understanding of what education systems should provide, and these can only be achieved through the incorporation of new actors in schools, other than teachers: not only psychologists, but pedagogues, social educators and social workers could be invited to join schools, not only schools attended by vulnerable people, but ordinary schools too. Either this can be done, or other institutions might be invited to join the educational task that school still rules as the monopoly it is.

Finally, the pandemic has given hints of certain features that schools might try to get rid of. The first one is, precisely, the monopoly of the right to education. If school systems accredit their sufficiency to educate the population and the ability to do so without the intervention of the families, the need to seek their cooperation during and after the lockdown has been a sign of the vulnerability of the school that, as an institution, has decreased in its legitimation in the past decades.

Another feature that may be put under scrutiny because of the pandemics is the rule of merit as the keystone for the school system. Success and failure do not have the same value nowadays, assessment has suffered variations and adaptations that have shown it does not need to be as rigid as it used to, and academic knowledge, the winner dimension during the lockdown, has seen other dimensions of education being valued and appreciated in the reopening of education.

Perhaps, a final remark can be made upon the hyper-responsibility of education in so many domains in the life of young people: the school is not able to cope with everything, it is not the only responsible of how people evolve, what they learn and how they develop and become adults.

The new normal is not necessarily the same as the old normal, distance education and digital education (particularly Artificial Intelligence) may become part of school insofar it adds value to face-to-face education, which has not been replaced. Digital means can perhaps achieve certain academic aims of education but that has not been the case with other goals. Digital means helped during the pandemic, but they have not been able to replace, only to complement face-to-face.

Education has recovered but it has changed, it has been restricted, it has returned to an altered population and society. Let me finish by wondering whether education, understood as school education, may be reconsidered, and what is essential of formal education in school practice, whether anything at all.

Further Reading

Castaño, J., Weikert, L., & Herrero, C. (2021). *Analysing the digital capacity of Spanish schools using SELFIE*. EUR 30735 EN, Publications Office of the European Union, Luxembourg, JRC125197. https://publications.jrc.ec.europa.eu/repository/handle/JRC125197, https://doi.org/10.2760/947402

Cedefop, (2020). *Digital gap during COVID-19 for VET learners at risk in Europe. Synthesis report on seven countries based on preliminary information provided by Cedefop's Network of Ambassadors tackling early leaving from VET*. https://www.cedefop.europa.eu/files/digital_gap_during_covid-19.pdf

CEPAL-UNESCO. (2020). *La educación en tiempos de la pandemia de COVID-19*. https://www.cepal.org/es/publicaciones/45904-la-educacion-tiempos-la-pandemia-covid-19

Coalición española Campaña Mundial por la Educación. (2020). *Proteger el derecho a la educación frente a la crisis del coronavirus*. CME-España. https://cme-espana.org/wp-content/uploads/2020/04/Posicionamiento-final.pdf

Consejo Escolar del Estado. (2021). *Situación actual de la educación en España a consecuencia de la pandemia*. https://www.educacionyfp.gob.es/mc/cee/publicaciones/estudios/situacion-pandemia.html

Davies, A. (2021). *Educación en tiempos de Covid-19*. Entreculturas. https://www.escuelarefugio.org/entreculturas/Educacion_en_tiempos_de_Covid19.pdf

Di Pietro, G., Biagi, F., Dinis Mota Da Costa, P., Karpinski, Z., & Mazza, J. (2020). *The likely impact of COVID-19 on education: Reflections based on the existing literature and recent international datasets*. EUR 30275 EN, Publications Office of the European Union, JRC121071.https://doi.org/10.2760/126686

Equipo estatal de educación de plena inclusion. (2020). *El derecho a la educación durante el Covid-19*. Plena Inclusión España. https://www.plenainclusion.org/sites/default/files/el_derecho_a_la_educacion_durante_el_covid19.pdf

Eurispes. (2022). *Covid 19—A journey into social precarity*. In Proceedings International Conference "Shifts and reorientationswithin the social crisis and pandemic catastrophe", promoted by the S.U.P.I. Network, international research group on Precariousness and Social Uncertainty in collaboration with the Italian institute Eurispes, 29–30 April 2021.

European Parliament, Directorate-General for Internal Policies of the Union, Dunajeva, J., Bankauskaite, R., Siarova, H., et al. (2021). *Education and youth in post-COVID-19 Europe: Crisis effects and policy recommendations*. European Parliament. https://doi.org/10.2861/047424

European Training Fund. (2020). *Coping with Covid-19. Mapping education and training responses to the health crisis in ETF partner countries*. ETF. https://www.etf.europa.eu/sites/default/files/2020-04/mapping_covid_060420_0.pdf

Fundación Secretariado Gitano. (2020). *Impacto de la crisis del Covid-19 sobre la población gitana*. FSGG. https://www.eapn.es/covid19/ARCHIVO/documentos/noticias/1587475880_1587475196_encuesta-participantes-fsg.pdf

German Office for International Cooperation in Vocational Education and Training. (2022). *Effects of the Covid-19 pandemic on vocational education and training: International perspectives of policy makers and practitioners*. Bibb. https://www.bibb.de/dienst/veroeffentlichungen/en/publication/show/17576

Gustafson, M. (2021). *Pandemic-related disruptions to schooling and impacts on learning proficiency indicators: A focus on the early grades*. UNESCO. http://uis.unesco.org/sites/default/files/documents/covid-19_interruptions_to_learning_-_final2.pdf

Hernández, F., Obiol, S., & Villar, A. (2020). *Innovació educativa del professorat valencià durant la Covid-19*. Universitat de València. https://roderic.uv.es/bitstream/handle/10550/75680/covid.pdf?sequence=1

Klette K., Sigurðardóttir, A. K., & Martin, H. (2021). Nordic values and schooling during COVID-19 how to balance comprehensive education and sustainable pandemic regulations. *Education in the North, 28*(3).

Lidegran, I., Hultqvist, E., Bertilsson, E., & Börjesson, M. (2021). Insecurity, lack of support, and frustration: A sociological analysis of how three groups of students reflect on their distance education during the pandemic in Sweden. *European Journal of Education, 0*, 1–14. https://doi.org/10.1111/ejed.12477

Martínez, M., Rodríguez, I., & Velásquez, G. (2020). *¿Cómo viven la situación de confinamiento niños, niñas y adolescentes? Infancia confinada y Enclave de evaluación.*

Mwesigwa, A. (2022). https://www.eldiario.es/desalambre/vuelta-cole-cierre-mundo-pandemia_1_8663196.html

OECD. (2020). Education at a glance 2020: OECD indicators. *OECD*. https://doi.org/10.1787/69096873-en

Reimers, F.M. (2022). Learning from a pandemic. The impact of COVID-19 on education around the world. In F. M. Reimers (eds.), *Primary and secondary education during Covid-19*. Springer. https://doi.org/10.1007/978-3-030-81500-4_1

UNESCO et al. (2021). *What's next? Lessons on education recovery: Findings from a survey of Ministries of Education amid the COVID-19 pandemic*. OECD Publishing., https://doi.org/10.1787/697bc36e-en.

UNICEF. (2021). *Covid-19 and school closures: One year of education disruption*. https://data.unicef.org/resources/one-year-of-covid-19-and-school-closures/

UNU-EHS & UNDDR Report. (2022). *Rethinking risks in times of Covid-19*. https://www.undrr.org/rethinking-risk-times-covid-19

Van der Graaf, L., Dunajeva, J., Siarova, H., & Bankauskaite, R. (2021). *Research for CULT Committee—Education and youth in post-COVID-19 Europe—Crisis effects and policy recommendations*. European Parliament, Policy Department for Structural and Cohesion Policies. https://www.europarl.europa.eu/RegData/etudes/STUD/2021/690872/IPOL_STU(2021)690872_EN.pdf

VV.AA. (2021). *Education in times of Coronavirus: Latin-American and the Caribbean education systems in the face of Covid-19*. Interamerican Development Bank. https://publications.iadb.org/en/education-times-coronavirus-latin-america-and-caribbeans-education-systems-face-covid-19, https://doi.org/10.18235/0002337

Zafra, I. (2022). *La avalancha de confinamientos escolares pone contra las cuerdas a las familias: "Estamos desesperadas"*. https://elpais.com/educacion/2022-01-21/la-avalancha-de-confinamientos-escolares-pone-contra-las-cuerdas-a-las-familias-estamos-desesperadas.html

Zafra, I. (2022). *Los alumnos de la escuela pública perdieron el equivalente a medio curso de Matemáticas por la pandemia y los de la concertada, apenas nada*. https://elpais.com/educacion/2022-03-16/los-alumnos-de-la-escuela-publica-perdieron-el-equivalente-a-medio-curso-de-matematicas-por-la-pandemia-y-los-de-la-concertada-apenas-nada.html

Zurriaga, O. (2022). *Cerrar colegios por la covid-19: una idea que no ha probado beneficios, pero sí daños*. The Conversation. https://theconversation.com/cerrar-colegios-por-la-covid-19-una-idea-que-no-ha-probado-beneficios-pero-si-danos-174995

A Fracture in a Broken Crystal: Artists' Precarity Under Crisis

António M. Duarte

Social sciences have identified that artistic work typically characterizes as highly precarious, both professionally, and creatively or ontologically (for a review see, for example, Duarte, 2020). As crises tend to increase social inequalities, artists, who are already exposed to high degrees of precarity and so much unprotected, along unskilled workers (Waite, 2009), tend to experience an increase of such precarity under those conditions. Therefore, crises might also reveal the most critical components of that precarity. Besides, since the social representation of artists' precarity, including the one of policy, is not so well clear than the one of research (Comunian & England, 2020), moments of crisis seem to have the power of increasing the social visibility of such precarity (Comunian & Conor, 2017), and of stressing the need for structural changes. All these aspects are in analogy with Sigmund Freud's metaphor for psychopathology: "If we throw a crystal to the floor, it breaks; but not into haphazard pieces. It comes apart along its lines of cleavage into fragments whose boundaries, though they were invisible, were predetermined by the crystal's structure." (Freud, 1933, p. 58). With more concrete relevance for the thematic of this chapter, Albert Camus also wrote, in his 1947 novel The Plague, "It was as if the earth on which our houses stood were being purged of its secreted humors; thrusting up to the surface the abscesses and pus-clots that had been forming in its entrails." (Camus, 1948, p. 16).

A. M. Duarte (✉)
Faculty of Psychology, University of Lisbon, Lisbon, Portugal
e-mail: amduarte@psicologia.ulisboa.pt

R. D. Hepp (ed.), *Shifts and Reorientation Within the Social-Crisis and Catastrophe: Towards the Realization of Pandemic Epistemological Processes*, Prekarisierung und soziale Entkopplung – transdisziplinäre Studien,
https://doi.org/10.1007/978-3-658-43041-2_6

Analysis of the impact of the COVID-19 pandemic crisis that started in 2020 on artists' precarity has therefore not only intrinsic value but is also an opportunity to draw attention to an already existing problem. The goal of this paper is to explore knowledge, gained so far in different national contexts, mostly by social sciences research, about impact of that pandemic crisis on artists' precarity. Besides, there is also focus on how some artists testified through their art a negative impact of the pandemic on their work, or somehow integrated this thematic in it, mostly in answering to art calls on the subject.

The chapter is structured in three parts. In part one a summary is given on how the pandemic crisis impacted both on artists' precarity (and more generally in cultural workers' precarity), both at the professional and the ontological level. In part two, an analysis is done mainly on the professional and psychological consequences of such impact. Finally, in the conclusion, besides a summary, some practical implications are drawn regarding ways of helping artists and improving the future of the art world.

Impact of COVID-19 Pandemic Crisis on Artists' Precarity

As expected, there is evidence from several national contexts that the pandemic crisis increased artists' precarity in general, threatening the sustainability of many. Moreover, this increase added to a previous one resulting from the economic crisis of 2008 (Banks, 2020). Besides, the pandemic crisis affected more artists of the performing arts, where direct and non-protected interaction with audiences is essential (Bataille et al., 2020), female artists (Dümcke, 2021; Pacella et al., 2021), and probably even more the ones that are beginning their careers, that belong to ethnic minorities and that live in poorer areas (Comunian & England, 2020).

Impact of COVID -19 Pandemic Crisis in Professional Precarity

Mainly by obliging to the closing of cultural institutions and canceling cultural events, the pandemic provoked a significant reduction of work activity in the cultural sector, especially in independent workers, in micro-firms and non-profit organizations, in the venue-based sub-sectors (e.g., festivals, live music, performing arts, cinema, museums, etc.), and all these in higher levels than in the general population (e.g., Kern, 2020; OECD, 2020). For example, 90 percent of world museums have closed during the pandemic crisis (UNESCO, 2020) and, emblematically, the Berlin Philharmonic Orchestra had never gone through such a long closure since its foundation in the 19th century, even during the world wars or the Spanish flu (Dümcke, 2021). More radically, in some contexts, like China, the pandemic crisis might have even eradicated, at least in the near future, some cultural events, like many independent music venues (Gu et al., 2021), and in the global context more than 10 percent of world museums may never reopen (UNESCO, 2020).

The impact of the pandemic in cultural work reduction is interpretable in a work for the call "Art in Quarantine", by Umbigo art magazine, where artist Fábio Colaço, presents a pair of shoes with a stone on top. In a joint legend it is written: "Untitled (heavy), 2020, is a sculpture built from a ready-made logic. This work can be read as a metaphor for the current situation, trapped by a social, political and economic stone, Sisyphus of the time in which we live." (https://fabiocolaco.com/untitled-heavy).

Correlatively to the reduction in cultural work, the pandemic provoked a fall in the income/revenues of the cultural sector, parallelly to many others (Milne, 2020), along with an intended dislocation of many artists out or towards the periphery of cultural urban centers (Eikhof, 2020). Moreover, the prediction for the medium term is that this negative effect of the pandemic crisis will last and could amplify, due to drop of demand and investment and funding in culture (OECD, 2020).

Convergently, in a work titled (Un)natural Virus, 2020, for the referred call "Art in Quarantine", artist Colin Ginks, presents a short video of an ATM machine that returns a long blank bank coupon (https://www.youtube.com/watch?v=lo1Tcm p69lA&ab_channel=UmbigoMagazine). Also for this call, the duo Sara and André, presented an untitled work consisting of an official independent art worker's provider form filled with apparently meaningless doodles (https://umbigomagazine.com/pt/blog/2020/06/27/arte-em-quarentena-sara-andre).

As it happened with the virus responsible for the pandemic, the scenario of an increased artists' precarity globalized, but also assumed local variants, analyzed through national studies.

Preliminary results of a survey study in Portugal (Neves et al., 2020–2022, as cited in Nadais, 2021) reported a triplication of absence of work, from five to 16 percent, among independent cultural workers between 2019 and 2020, during the first pandemic wave. Furthermore, this is in heavy contrast with general unemployment during the same period, that reached a maximum of eight percent. Parallelly, in Portugal some artistic sectors were particularly more affected by the pandemic crisis, like the one of performance (Borges, 2020) and urban artists (Ferro, 2020).

A survey study in Malta (Visanich & Attard, 2020) indicated that 90.8 percent of artists' working activities, like exhibitions, concerts, and performances, were cancelled (52.8 %) or postponed (38.0 %) due to the pandemic. Moreover, for these artists much of their work was not transferable online, since many are freelancers that work from temporary projects, provoking a significant negative impact on their income (Visanich & Attard, 2020).

Studies on the situation in Germany (Dümke, 2021) also indicated a significant reduction in artist's working activity and correspondent revenues. Consequently, it was previewed that the cultural and creative sectors will lose between 12.7 and 23 percent of their annual return due to the pandemic crisis (Dümke, 2021).

A meta-analysis of survey studies conducted in UK (Comunian & England, 2020) indicated a significant reduction of organizational activities and individual workloads in the creative and cultural sector, in many cases of 100 percent (Comunian & England, 2020). Artists were particularly affected by this, with 82 percent of respondents having their work canceled (like events, performances, and public activities), due to official advice to social distance and self-isolation. Additionally, the crisis might provoke a long-term breakdown of freelance work provision, from which many artists depend as a secondary income source. Furthermore, the long-term impact of the crisis on artistic work activity might be bigger in sectors where audiences could take longer to gain security for attending performances or events. Naturally, the UK reduction in work activity also corresponded to a significant loss of income/revenue for organizations and individuals working in the creative and cultural sector (Comunian & England, 2020).

According to a US report (Randy, 2021) American artists/creatives belong to the working group that is was most affected in terms of reduction of work activity due to the pandemic. Specifically, in the beginning of March 2021 they were experiencing a reduction of 79 percent in creative work that generates income, with 62 percent with "drastic decrease". Consequently, those artists/creatives reported a loss of income of 95 percent. Moreover, from those, "black, indigenous, artists of color" were suffering more than white artists.

A study on the situation in Argentina (Serafini & Novosel, 2021) reported that 44 percent of the workers in the cultural sector had their activities and income suspended due to the pandemic crisis. Besides, 32 percent of those were unable to pay basic personal expenses.

A study that analysis the impact of the pandemic crisis in the cultural industries of the African continent (Joffe, 2021) points to their drastic decline due to the imposed restrictions, despite their relative underdevelopment.

A study on the impact of the pandemic crisis in Australian music industry (Brunt & Nelligan, 2020) indicated radical reduction in Australian musicians' work activity due to the national closure of live music venues in March 2020. Consequently, the music industry lost millions in that country.

Consistently with and corroborating the reduction in their work activity and income, artists publicly manifested and informed on the intensification of their precarity, and at the same time required support.

For instance, in UK there was an active requirement of government support by organizations and individuals working in the creative and cultural sector, frequently by lobby, in face of the increased precarity the pandemic brought (Comunian & England, 2020). Specific required actions included tax suspension, rent holidays, interest-free loans, faster access to funding, grants and simplifying applications for Universal Credit. Similarly, in US artists/creatives reported a need of food/housing assistance, forgivable business loans, and unemployment insurance (Randy, 2021).

In a performance, by Nuno Gama and Olga Roriz (2020), that took place in a public space in Lisbon, instead of presenting clothes, fashion models only dressed black thongs (https://visao.sapo.pt/atualidade/sociedade/2020-10-10-nuno-gama-mostrou-performance-em-vez-de-colecao-na-modalisboa).

Impact of COVID -19 Pandemic Crisis on Ontological Precarity

The professional limitations brought by the pandemic to the artists resulted also in non-previewed changes to their creative work, in ways that constrained it and even alienated it.

Imposed social distancing due to the pandemic was a condition in antinomy with the experience of direct exhibition and contact with art works (Horváth, 2020). The consequence was an impossibility of such exhibition and art appreciation or a reduction in its quality, that became dependent of an indirect showing and contact through art reproductions or streaming. Social distance measures, along with occasional closing of locals and events of art exhibition and performance, resulted then in a kind of "pandemic censorship" for the artists and their works. Moreover, in some cases these restrictions imposed changes in the works of art. For instance, the referred study in Malta, by Visanich and Attard (2020), indicated that although most cultural events were canceled or postponed due to the pandemic, some (5.2 %) shifted online, and others (3.9 %) changed due to it (specially rehearsals, work-in-progress, and creative research).

The "pandemic censorship" on art is represented by the work Memorial #2, of Nuno Vieira, 2020, presented to the previously referred call "Art in Quarantine": an empty room of art gallery with an office chair from the artist's studio, on which a room sheet is placed. The sheet had information about the works developed for the room but that remained stored in the artist's studio during the exhibition (https://umbigomagazine.com/pt/blog/2020/04/10/arte-em-quarentena-nuno-sousa-vieira/). Another work in the same direction, produced to the same call, is Still-life Agitable #2, 2020, by Diogo Costa, that shows a work of art inside a box (https://umbigomagazine.com/pt/blog/2020/05/15/arte-em-quarentena-diogo-costa/).

Paradoxically, this production of art works that refer to the pandemic crisis, along with others that contribute to recommend health safety and adaptative personal/social practices during this crisis (e.g., Adenle & Akande, 2020; Buchmiller et al., 2020; Pandanwangi et al., 2021), show again not only the resilience of art under negative conditions, but also that art finds new forms and motives under those conditions, which serves as a way of articulating and coping with them (e.g., Govinden, 2020). Convergently, forced confinement due to the pandemic increased the amount and reduced the costs of the offer to culture and art, through television and internet, and turned more people into it, both in terms of appreciation and creation, testifying and increasing the visibility of its importance in public well-being (Banks, 2020; OECD, 2020). Nevertheless, there is also a risk in this boom: the reinforcement of a social representation of art as a mere source of joy or relaxation, in oblivion to its needed function in social critique (Banks, 2020; Martinho, 2020).

It should also be considered that the pandemic crisis brought perceived advantages to the creative work of some (maybe established) artists: for instance, some (like Portuguese sculptor Rui Chafes) reported that the forced confinement during the pandemic worked as an opportunity of reclusion and social isolation that allowed them to concentrate exclusively and satisfactorily in their work (de Oliveira, 2021). A fact that is not surprising considering isolation is a common working routine among artists (Currey, 2013). Moreover, this converges with some of the results of a study that compared 235 social sciences students' diaries pre and during the pandemic and lockdown: "little-c level" or "everyday" creative activity (including artistic creativity of the same level) significantly increased during lockdown (Karwowski et al., 2021). The authors hypothesise that creative activity during lockdown might serve as an emotion regulation strategy to relieve boredom, keep oneself busy and improve the mood. Actually, some research founded evidence that social isolation and sensory deprivation can benefit creativity (e.g., Forgays & Forgays. 1992), maybe because those conditions can promote daydreaming, which frequently characterizes as creative (Arieti, 1976). Additionally, economic and social crises can be periods with positive impact in art production, even provoking new art movements, like expressionism and modernism (Radermercker, 2021).

Oppositely, for some artists reclusion and social isolation are counterproductive. For instance, due to the forced confinement, performer artists and students dependent of a workspace in-person coaching to maintain and develop technical and artistic abilities, like circus artists, risk falling behind their labor force in the expected pos-confinement phase (Stuckey et al., 2021). According to these authors this could result that those in such condition might seek different employment pathways.

Furthermore, due to the impact of the pandemic crisis on closing borders and limiting international travel cultural exchange and cross-cultural learning opportunities, such as artistic residences and tours abroad, was restricted (Global Impact, 2020, as cited in Anheier et al. 2021).

A relevant art testimony is a work, by urban artist MaisMenos, 2020, composed of the graffiti sentence New World Border (which gives the title to the work), sprayed on a window blind (https://www.artsy.net/artwork/plus-maismenos-plus-new-world-border). While the work can intentionally allude to the special tragedy of the forced home confinement of urban artists, it is also interpretable as a reference to the within borders enclosing of artists and people in general.

Consequences of Artists' Precarity Increment

Increment of artists' precarity due to the pandemic crisis had several consequences regarding sustainability and pursuit of art careers, the adaption of new required form of artistic work, mental health and well-being, and support availability.

Due to the pandemic crisis some artists and cultural workers were obliged to leave their profession, which can derive in the loss of talent for society (Anheimer et al., 2021). The crisis might also have a long-term impact of reducing the motivation and financial support students need to enter higher education in the arts, by increasing the difficulties art graduates will have in joining the sector (Comunian et al., 2020).

Besides, by imposing artists and artistic institutions with their audiences the pandemic crisis pusheed an online shift of art exhibition in the form of online museum displays, virtual exhibitions, distant visits, virtual events, and streaming (Gu et al., 2021; Horváth, 2020). The crisis therefore reduced a collective, physical, on site, indoor, public pattern of art consumption and increased a digital/virtual, private, home, free and open-access pattern (Radermecker, 2021). In this way the crisis might also had stimulated the development of virtual ways of displaying art or of complementing the real exhibition of art in the post-pandemic future. For instance, virtual exhibitions facilitate the availability of art by overcoming physical restrictions and complement and increase the impact of physical exhibitions, by extending audiences' motivation, deepening and participation (Foo, 2008). Some projects focused in expanding established ways of exhibiting art, by creating paired digital contexts (Marmeleira, 2021). Besides, such development will also prospectively benefit persons generally or occasionally limited to an exclusive virtual contact with art or with some art works (e.g., individuals with special needs, isolated or in a long-distance).

But despite allowing a virtual display and a form of accessibility to some art this online shift of art is also problematic, since it does not properly compensate the lack of direct delivery. Primarily, only 54 percent of the word population has access to internet (The State of Broadband, 2020, as cited in Anheier et al. 2021), and with unequal media literacy competencies (Quintela & Rodrigues, 2020). Also, the online shift can compromise a fair gain and control by artists for their digital displays (CuttingEdge, 2020, as cited in Anheier et al. 2021). Such shift is not possible or easy to all artistic activities and systems, functioning as an "unequalizer" (Anheier et al. 2021). Effectively, the need to digitalize and transfer artistic content online requires costly training and time of work that can discriminate many artists which will be left behind (Comunian & England, 2020). For example, the augmented consumption of streamed cultural content during lockdown benefited the main specialized companies (OECD, 2020). The prolonged use of digital tools that the online shift is also demanding from artists can provoke exhaustion and a longing for manual crafty work (Marmeleira, 2021). The mass availability during forced confinements of much art works in an open access mode also developed audiences' expectations that such works should be accessible for "minimal or low cost" (CuttingEdge, 2020, as cited in Anheier et al. 2021). Furthermore, the exclusive virtual and distant contact with art can change and probably limits the process of art appreciation. Most importantly, that kind of contact simply does not replace the real contact with art, and some forms of art are not prone to digitalization (Polivsteva, 2020). Plus, such online contact might lead audiences to surf across reproductions of works of art and to spend only a short time on specific ones (Anheier et al. 2021). Virtual and distant contact with works of art also limits the behavioral dimension of art appreciation. As an art spectator testifies: "(…) I just cannot connect, it's not natural. For example, let us say that tomorrow the Cinematheque shows a movie at 22:00. My body must dislocate there. There is a deliberation, an agency that does not occur in the digital." (Marmeleira, 2021, p. 20). Finally, the rapid online shift of art might somehow also be conceptualized as a symptom of an economical expansionism that even exploits the pandemic, still if involuntarily, and might threaten the quality of art appreciation (Quintela & Rodrigues, 2020).

In a performance named Cuarentena de Impresión (Printing Quarentine), within the larger project Impresiones sobre Actualidad (Impressions on Actuality), 2020, Colombian artist José Diaz confined in an art gallery, lively broadcasting 24 h. per day, to continue printing sentences on the actuality, some of which expose the constrains the pandemic brought on artistic work (e.g.," Today, at a distance"; "Today, virtual") (González-Martin, 2021) (www.espacioeldorado.com/impresiones-sobre-actualidad).

A more specific form of artists' ontological precarity the pandemic crisis and the online shift indirectly promoted derives from the fact that such seems to stimulate the "criptoart" market (Pequenino, 2021), which involves transactions (with criptocoins) of digital art or digital registries of works of art (and not the works themselves), possibly made by the artists, known as "non-fungible tokens - NFTs".

Criptoart seems to present some advantages for the artists, like the increase of visibility (particularly relevant during pandemic), the register of works' chains of provenience, the possible gain for in subsequent sales, and some independence from intermediaries (Pequenino, 2021). Nevertheless, as this author states, criptoart also facilitates certain forms of artists' alienation, like non-authorised NFTs upon works of art, or use of worthless criptocoins in their transaction. Moreover, NFTs seem to promote art speculation and instrumentalization: for instance, a work of art (Morons, by Banksy, 2016, which ironically represents an art auction) was already bought, digitalized, and destroyed in order to increase the value of its correspondent NFT (Criddle, 2021).

Besides, as one of the potential consequences of professional precarity is the deterioration of mental health and well-being (Blustein et al., 2016), it can be expected that an increased precarity due to the crisis will also increase such deterioration, also possibly amplified by confinement and social distancing. In his participation on the Wreading-digits' "Art in Quarentine" call, 2020, artist Jan Theuninck presented a photo of himself as a prostrated, apparently depressed, street beggar near a written sign Exiled in my own Country, which also gives the title to the work.

Most of the inquired artists in the study of Visanich and Attard (2020), in Malta, indicated that the effects of the pandemic on work termination and postponement had a significant impact on their life satisfaction and well-being. In the same direction, an analysis of media narratives about the Australian music industry's mental health crisis that have emerged during the pandemic (Brunt & Nelligan, 2020), suggested that many musicians were traumatically experiencing loss, grief, anxiety, and despair, provoked by absence of work, with significant impact on their mental health. Parallelly, the same analysis disclosed a correlatively increase of promotion about wellbeing resources for musicians (e.g., self-care tips, counselling, psychotherapy).

Moreover, particularly for artists that could not transfer their workspace to their home context, like performers, the pandemic crisis created new stressors that can amplify even more mental health problems (Stuckey et al., 2021). As these authors state, since performer artists ground their work on the body and on the interaction with the context, including apparatus and audience (making their art bodily extended and embodied), they are more psychologically vulnerable to a forced separation of material/social spaces.

Nevertheless, it should be considered that deterioration of mental health and well-being in artists that are able to keep creating might be partly compensated by the know positive effects art activities have on mental health, in terms of lowering anxiety and depression, and of increasing life satisfaction (Randy, 2021).

The pronunciation of artists' precarity due to the pandemic crisis prompted some cities and states to support artists and culture workers and organizations with measures like subsidies or tax delays or rebates (Anheier et al. 2021; Betzler et al., 2020; Brian & O'Connor, 2021b; Dümcke, 2021; Joffe, 2021; Pacella et al., 2021; Serafini & Novosel, 2020). Such support was justified not only by the need of helping a collapsing sector, but also considering the psychological, social, and economic functions of art and culture (Brian & O'Connor, 2021b). Nevertheless, besides the fact that the scale and scope of this support varied much across and within contexts (Anheier et al. 2021; Brian & O'Connor, 2021b), in many even this support problems and obstacles. In general, much of this support is not adequate to the freelance, intermittent and hybrid work of the artists (OECE, 2020). Further, most support was given to institutions and their employees, rather to individual artists, that often are ineligible freelancers (Anheier et al. 2021). For instance, in UK newly employed cultural workers did not received government support since this requires a record of tax returns (Comunian & England, 2020). In Portugal the pandemic crisis leaved many cultural workers without social support (e.g., layoff; unemployment budget), since their condition as precarious (e.g., working without a contract) was not making them eligible to such support (Carvalho & Sousa, 2021), a fact that triggered structural reforms in this issue. The equivalent happened in Australia, since many arts and culture workers fail the prerequisite of a 12-month continuous employment with one employer (Pacella et al., 2021). Considering the obstacles to an effective general support to artists in need independently of their status, it has been argued that the crisis likely increased the winner-take-all structures in cultural markets (Betzler, et al., 2020). More importantly, it seems that state support of the cultural sector in face of the pandemic crisis consisted mainly of emergency reactions, in the absence of a needed strategic action that would contribute for a longer-term improvement of its conditions (Serafini, & Novosel, 2021).

Conclusion

Like crises in general, the COVID-19 pandemic crisis seemed to increase the already existing precarity that tends to affect artists, as many other disadvantaged workers, promoting the social inequality they tend to be exposed to. Consequently, this crisis seemed to make more visible an higher precarity that artists already tended to be exposed to, and that does not result from it. In this perspective, the specific impact of this crisis on artists' precarity can be placed in a more general context of a crisis of neoliberalism (Banks, 2020; Banks & Connor, 2021b; Meyrick & Barnett, 2020) or of "rentier capitalism", if we better consider that economy has evolved to such a scenario (Standing, 2020).

Having in mind that the exploratory analysis here conducted is mostly based on ongoing research that just delivered early findings, it is possible to conclude that the pandemic crisis increased artists' typical, although heterogeneous, shortage of work activity, and low income. This is naturally accompanied by artists' public denouncement of their situation and claim for official support. Moreover, by distancing art/artists and audiences (beneficial for some artists and unsuitable for others) the crisis brought a kind of "pandemic censorship" of art, that nevertheless resisted trough a (potentially advantageous, but problematic) online shift, a development of new themes and a contribution to the global response against the pandemic. Besides, confinement of artists threatened the creative sustainability and development of some. Consequently, the crisis might have sabotaged vocational orientation to the arts and maintenance of art careers, demanded digital work adaptations for which not all artists are prepared, might have increased in them the deterioration of mental health and well-being that typically results from precarity, and prompted unequal state support for which many artists are ineligible.

For the short-term, the pandemic crisis demanded ways of helping artists in need, especially the ones in this condition who just live from artistic work. In this line several actions have been proposed for artists (Joffe, 2021; OECD, 2020; Visanich & Attard, 2020) like: emergency funds, in the logic of the universal basic income; solidarity grants; quick resolution of pending payments; advanced payment of new commissions; tax incentives; or investment in cultural production. Besides, counselling and psychotherapy services and resources can be facilitated, to help artists dealing with the pandemic impact on personal mental health (e.g., Stuckey et al, 2021). Moreover, artists can be assisted on how to connect with their audiences and produce revenue at a distance (e.g., online exhibiting; livestreaming; etc.). Digitalization of art and culture demands development of digital skills in artists, greater extensibility of digital access (OECD, 2020), and adequate ground and planning (Quintela & Rodrigues, 2020), by artists and cultural workers (Polivtseva, 2020), in order its quality is not threaten.

For the long-term the pandemic crisis stresses the need to: find ways of making free-lance artists eligible to special social security measures in case of need, like wage-supplements or layoff (Visanich and Attard, 2020); reinforce the importance that artists organize in cooperatives (Battaile et al., 2020) and lobby groups that represent them collectively; invest in digital infrastructure (OECD, 2020); and to promote intersection of culture with education and health services (OECD, 2020).

Moreover, this crisis stresses the need, potentially constituting an opportunity, for structural actions that help to reduce or eradicate artists' precarity in the future and not only in the short-term. Basic income can be one answer to artists' precarity, and for precarity in general, as the following quote of a testimony of an artist illustrates:

"We are all emotional beings as well as rational ones. My basic income payment was the day I became free – a signal I could dream of something better" (Standing, 2020, p. 94). But aspiring for more, this crisis is an opportunity for developing conditions of stable and adequately remunerated work for artists (Comunian & England, 2020), along with due social care (Quintela & Rodrigues, 2020), under a possible "new deal for culture" (Banks & O'Connor, 2021a, p. 1). Furthermore, this crisis appeals to the need of developing cultural infrastructures and seriously assuming the social role of culture and arts, parallelly to other social components like sports or health (Anheier et al., 2021). This would dignify art and artistic work and would develop its sustainability in general and in the face of future crises. As other previous crises, the pandemic crisis stresses therefore the social regard owned to the artists, and that seems expressed in the work Self Portrait of the Artist during COVID-19, by Chris Theiss, 2020, a bust of himself using a respirator mask, inside a glass bell, with the word "respect" at the base.

Besides, the crisis opens the opportunity to move beyond a massive tourism-based culture to models that favor cross-innovation between the cultural sector and traditional manufacturing and services; and to use culture to raise awareness on structural threats like climate change and population ageing (OECD, 2020).

Finalizing, the negative impact of this pandemic crisis in artists, as in the other sectors, can be treated with palliative care, just to return, after the pandemic, to the previous situation or, alternatively, with measures that help to restructure the relationship of artists and other workers with society. In a series entitled The Ghostlight Theatre Project, for the exhibition "Art in the Plague Year", by California Museum of Photography, 2021, artist Sara Boyer presents a sequence of photos of vacant theatres, illuminated by "ghost lights", that she visited during the pandemic across Southern California. As the exhibition text that accompanies this series states: "The project, however, is not about emptiness but potential. After all, an empty theater is pure possibility. Theater is a site of change. "When we are invited back in, theater will have evolved. It will invite more of us back in to all its phases—audience, creatives, actors, stagehands, stories. It will be stronger. That is what theater does. That is what we do." And we ourselves will be changed. Theater is "where we transform," states the artist." (California Museum of Photography, 2021).

References

Adenle, J. O., & Akande, A. (2020). The artists in pandemic, pandemic in arts: Artistic responses to the ripples of Covid-19 in Nigeria. *KIU Journal of Humanities, 5*(3), 237–247. http://www.ijhumas.com/ojs/index.php/kiuhums/article/view/1041

Anheier, H. K., Merkel, J., & Winkler, K. (2021). *Culture, the arts and the COVID-19 pandemic: Five cultural capitals in search of solutions*. Hertie School. https://doi.org/10.48462/opus4-3722

Arieti, S. (1976). Creativity: *The magic synthesis*. Basic Books.

Banks, M. (2020). The work of culture and C-19. *European Journal of Cultural Studies, 23*(4), 648–654. https://doi.org/10.1177/1367549420924687

Banks, M., & O'Connor, J. (2021). Editorial: Art and culture in the viral emergency. *Cultural Trends, 30*(1), 1–2. https://doi.org/10.1080/09548963.2021.1882063

Banks, M., & O'Connor, J. (2021). "A plague upon your howling": Art and culture in the viral emergency. *Cultural Trends, 30*(1), 3–18. https://doi.org/10.1080/09548963.2020.1827931

Bataille, P., Bertolini, S., Casula, C., & Perrenoud, M. (2020). Artistic work in pandemic times. *Sociologia del Lavoro, 157*, 55–58. https://doi.org/10.3280/SL2020-157003

Betzler, D., Loots, E., Prokůpek, M., Marques, L., & Prafenauer, P. (2020). COVID-19 and the arts and cultural sectors: Investigating countries' contextual factors and early policy measures. *International Journal of Cultural Policy*. https://doi.org/10.1080/10286632.2020.1842383

Blustein, D. L., Olle, C., Connors-Kellgren, A., Diamonti, A. J., Sartori, R., & Pouyaud, J. (2016). Decent work: A psychological perspective. *Frontiers in Psychology, 7*, 407. https://doi.org/10.3389/fpsyg.2016.00407

Borges, V. (2020). O trabalho nas artes performativas na era COVID-19: Da urgência ao potencial da mudança nas organizações e nas trajetórias de carreira artísticas (Work in the performing arts in the COVID-19 era: From urgency to the potential of change in organizations and artistic career trajectories). In T. Leão (Ed.) *Em suspenso. Reflexões sobre o trabalho artístico, cultural e criativo na era COVID-19* [On hold. Reflections on artistic, cultural and creative work in the COVID-19 era] (pp. 31–40). Universidade do Porto.

Brunt, S., & Nelligan, K. (2020). The Australian music industry's mental health crisis: Media narratives during the coronavirus pandemic. *Media International Australia*, 1329878X20948957. https://doi.org/10.1177/1329878X20948957

Buchmiller, M., Annable, G,. Fox, E., Hinkley, E., LeDoux, J. Sugiuchi, E. S., Surrey, E. Tony, T., & Timke, E. (2020). Erase COVID: An interview with artists creating PSAs to take on a global pandemic. *Advertising & Society Quarterly, 21*(2). https://doi.org/10.1353/asr.2020.0019

California Museum of Photography. (2021). *Art in the plague year*. https://www.artintheplagueyear.com/Sara-Jane-Boyers

Camus, A. (1948). *The plague*. Translated by S. Gilbert. Random House.

Carvalho M., & de Sousa, T. (2021, March 5). *Esta crise foi o maior atestado de falhanço das visões neoliberais* [This crisis was the biggest proof of failure of the neoliberal visions]. Publico. https://www.publico.pt/2021/03/04/politica/noticia/crise-maior-atestado-falhanco-visoes-neoliberais-1953076

Comunian, R., & Conor, B. (2017). Making cultural work visible in cultural policy. In V. Durrer, T. Miller, & D. O'Brien (Eds.), *The Routledge handbook of global cultural policy* (pp. 265–280). Routledge.

Comunian, R., Dent, T., & England, L. (2020, April 29). *Creative higher education and Covid-19*. www.creativeHEcovid.org/blog

Comunian, R., & England, L. (2020). Creative and cultural work without filters: Covid-19 and exposed precarity in the creative economy. *Cultural Trends, 29*(2), 112–128. https://doi.org/10.1080/09548963.2020.1770577

Criddle, C. (2021, March 9). *Banksy art burned, destroyed and sold as token in 'money-making stunt'*. BBC. https://www.bbc.com/news/technology-56335948

Currey, M. (2013). *Daily rituals*. Knopf.

De Oliveira, L. S. (2021, March 19). *O que me passa pela cabeça* [What's on my mind] (p. 31). Ypsilom.

Duarte, A. M. (2020). Artists' precarity in the context of their social integration. In T. Rachwał, R. Hepp, & D. Kergel (Eds.), *Precarious places: Social, cultural and economic aspects of uncertainty and anxiety in everyday life* (pp. 19–39). Springer.

Dümcke, C. (2021). Five months under COVID-19 in the cultural sector: A German perspective. *Cultural Trends, 30*(1), 19–27. https://doi.org/10.1080/09548963.2020.1854036

Eikhof, D. R. (2020). COVID-19, inclusion and workforce diversity in the cultural economy: What now, what next? *Cultural Trends, 29*(3), 234–250. https://doi.org/10.1080/09548963.2020.1802202

Ferro, L. (2020). A arte urbana na encruzilhada da pandemia: Reflexões sobre o trabalho cultural e artístico num segmento emergente [Urban art at the crossroads of the pandemic: Reflections on cultural and artistic work in an emerging segment]. In T. Leão (Ed.) *Em suspenso. Reflexões sobre o trabalho artístico, cultural e criativo na era COVID-19* [On hold. Reflections on artistic, cultural and creative work in the COVID-19 era] (pp. 57–67). Universidade do Porto.

Foo, S. (2008). Online virtual exhibitions: Concepts and design considerations. *Journal of Library and Information Technology, 28*(4), 22–34.

Forgays, D. G., & Forgays, D. K. (1992). Creativity enhancement through flotation isolation. *Journal of Environmental Psychology, 12*(4), 329–335. https://doi.org/10.1016/S0272-4944(05)80081-7

Freud, S. (1933). *The standard edition of the complete psychological works of Sigmund Freud, Volume XXII (1932–1936): New introductory lectures on psycho-analysis and other works* (trans. James Strachey). The Hogarth Press and the Institute of Psycho-Analysis.

González-Martín, C. (2021). El 'hoy' confinado en una galería de arte. Entrevista a José Ruiz (The "today" confined to an art gallery. Interview with José Ruiz). *Arte, Individuo Y Sociedad, 33*(2), 621–627. https://doi.org/10.5209/aris.70757

Govinden, B. (2020). The arts in the time of pandemic. *Agenda, 34*(2), 148–153. https://doi.org/10.1080/10130950.2020.1783888

Gu, X., Domer, N., & O'Connor, J. (2021). The next normal: Chinese indie music in a post-COVID China. *Cultural Trends, 30*(1), 63–64. https://doi.org/10.1080/09548963.2020.1846122

Horváth, G. (2020). Mine the gap. Fine arts in the age of pandemics In G. Horváth & R. K. Bakó (Eds.), *Mind the Gap! Proceedings of the Sixth Argumentor Conference 2020* (pp. 229–241). Debrecen University Press. https://philarchive.org/rec/HORMTG-2?all_versions=1

Joffe, A. (2021). Covid-19 and the African cultural economy: An opportunity to reimagine and reinvigorate? *Cultural Trends, 30*(1), 28–29. https://doi.org/10.1080/09548963.2020.1857211

Karwowski, M., Zielińska, A., Jankowska, D. M, Strutyńska, E., Omelańczuk, I., & Lebuda, I. (2021). Creative lockdown? A daily diary study of creative activity during pandemics. *Frontiers in Psychology, 12*(600076). https://doi.org/10.3389/fpsyg.2021.600076

Kern, P. (2020). *The impact of the COVID-19 pandemic on the cultural and creative sector*. Council of Europe. https://keanet.eu/wp-content/uploads/Impact-of-COVID-19-pandemic-on-CCS_COE-KEA_26062020.pdf.pdf

Martinho, T. D. (2020). Cultura, política, trabalho: Profissionais desocultados procuram direitos e cuidados [Culture, politics, work: Unhidden professionals seek rights and care]. In T. Leão (Ed.), *Em suspenso. Reflexões sobre o trabalho artístico, cultural e criativo na era COVID-19* [On hold. Reflections on artistic, cultural and creative work in the COVID-19 era] (pp. 7–14). Universidade do Porto.

Marmeleira, J. (2021, March 12). *Retratos de uma arte no limiar do digital* [Portraits of an art at the digital threshold] (pp. 16–20). Ípsilom.

Milne, A. K. L. (2020, March 21). *A critical COVID-19 economic policy tool: Retrospective insurance*. https://ssrn.com/abstract=3558667

Nadais. I. (2021, March 10). *Trabalho independente na cultura tende a ser precário (quando existe) (Independent work in culture tends to be precarious (when it exists))* (p. 30). Publico.

OECD. (2020). *Culture shock: COVID-19 and the cultural and creative sectors*. OECD. https://read.oecd-ilibrary.org/view/?ref=135_135961-nenh9f2w7a&title=Culture-shock-COVID-19-and-the-cultural-and-creative-sectors

Pacella, J., Luckman, S., & O'Connor, J. (2021). Fire, pestilence and the extractive economy: Cultural policy after cultural policy. *Cultural Trends, 30*(1), 40–51. https://doi.org/10.1080/09548963.2020.1833308

Pandanwangi, A., Dewi, B. S., Damayanti, N. Y., & Apin, A. M. (2021). *The impact of a pandemic to be strengthening artist tolerance in facing C-19 through digital art*. In Proceedings of the 3rd International Conference on Arts and Design Education - ICADE 2020 (pp. 83–87). Atlantis Press. https://doi.org/10.2991/assehr.k.210203.018

Pequenino, K. (2021, March 21). *A pandemia atraiu muitos para o curioso mundo da criptoarte (The pandemic has attracted many to the curious world of cryptoart)* (pp. 26–27). Público.

Polivtseva, E. (2020). *Live arts in the virtualisation world. IETM*. https://www.ietm.org/en/system/files/publications/live_arts_in_the_virtualising_world.pdf

Quintela, P., & Rodrigues, V. (2020). Pandemia e cultura: (Ainda) a urgência de um pensamento lento. In T. Leão (Ed.) *Em suspenso. Reflexões sobre o trabalho artístico, cultural e criativo na era COVID-19 (On hold. Reflections on artistic, cultural and creative work in the COVID-19 era)* (pp. 15–25). Universidade do Porto.

Radermecker, A. S. V. (2021). Art and culture in the COVID-19 era: For a consumer-oriented approach. *SN Business & Economics, 1*(4). https://doi.org/10.1007/s43546-020-00003-y

Randy, C. (2021, February 22). *COVID-19 Pandemic impact on the arts: Research update*. https://www.americansforthearts.org/node/103614

Serafini, P., & Novosel, N. (2021). Culture as care: Argentina's cultural policy response to Covid-19. *Cultural Trends, 30*(1), 52–62. https://doi.org/10.1080/09548963.2020.1823821

Standing, G. (2020). *Battling eight giants. Basic income now*. Tauris.

Stuckey, M., Richard, V., Decker, A., Aubertin, P., & Kriellaars, D. (2021). Supporting holistic wellbeing for performing artists during the COVID-19 pandemic and recovery: Study protocol. *Frontiers in Psychology, 12*(577882). https://doi.org/10.3389/fpsyg.2021.577882

UNESCO. (2020). *Museums around the world in the face of COVID-19*. https://unesdoc.unesco.org/ark:/48223/pf0000373530

Visanich, V., & Attard, T. (2020). Performing precarity in times of uncertainty: The implications of Covid-19 on artists in Malta. In J. M. Ryan (Ed.), *COVID-19. Volume II: Social consequences and cultural adaptations* (pp. 198-212). Routledge.

Waite, L. (2009). A place and space for a critical geography of precarity? *Geography Compass, 3*(1), 412–433. https://doi.org/10.1111/j.1749-8198.2008.00184.x

Precarity: Eclipsing the Face of the Other

Ronald C. Arnett

1 A Precarious Sentiment: Eclipsing the Face of the Other

As one engages the work of Emmanuel Levinas (1906–1995), a basic structure emerges. Levinas provides a phenomenological reminder of an immemorial ethical calling that commences with the face of the Other. Otherwise than Heidegger, Levinas offers ethics as a primordial call, prior to Being itself. Ethics, for Levinas, dwells within a revelatory reminder initiated in the meeting of the face of the Other. Encountering the face of the Other, for Levinas, is impersonal; his ethics expands beyond family, friendship, and locality. The face of the Other met impersonally moves one from a visual ethic to an audio call to responsibility: "I am my brother's keeper" (Levinas, 1998, p. 117). This audio call returns one to the Other in an act of responsibility that is particular and unique. Note that Levinas's ethics is universal, an audio call. The return to responsibility, however, is dependent upon the individual person(s) that claim one's attention and responsibility.

This ethical template hinges on one basic phenomenological glance. One must acknowledge and respond to the immediacy of the face of the Other without personal involvement. For Levinas, there are two basic modes of responsibility omission. First, one can attend only to those close in proximity and familiarity. Second, one can completely ignore the reality of the person in one's immediate

R. C. Arnett (✉)
Duquesne University Pittsburgh, Pittsburgh, PA, USA
e-mail: ronald.arnett@gmail.com

R. D. Hepp (ed.), *Shifts and Reorientation Within the Social-Crisis and Catastrophe: Towards the Realization of Pandemic Epistemological Processes*, Prekarisierung und soziale Entkopplung – transdisziplinäre Studien,
https://doi.org/10.1007/978-3-658-43041-2_7

presence. This essay attends primarily to the second omission—ignoring the face of the immediate Other. Levinas's orientation is akin to a routine stop sign; it only works when acknowledged, recognized, and followed.

The failure of comprehension of an immediate Other offers a lament-filled explanation of the Holocaust. Levinas lost his entire family, with the exception of his wife and daughter, to acts of execution in his hometown of Kaunas, Lithuania. Levinas, as a political prisoner from France, lived in prisoner-of-war camps for five years. During this time, he began his first major tome, Totality and Infinity: An Essay on Exteriority (1961). In this work, he offers a picture of ethics during a time of expanding atrocity. Levinas's project is a phenomenological rendering of human dwelling. The limits of his work manifest in the fact that he describes the call of ethics that comes without pristine clarity of direction. Levinas reminds us of a world that is parallel to an empirical world of acquisition. Levinas articulates an impressionistic picture of a social responsibility that is fundamental to the human spirit. Phenomenologically, each human being is derivative. Thus, the phrase "I am my brother's keeper" is a pragmatic, phenomenological reminder of a responsibility for the Other that ultimately impacts the quality of one's own life. As a derivative creature, I am, each one of us is, responsive to the Other. We are shaped by persons, environments, stories, practices, and ideas. Only in modernity, with its obsession with distance from social environments and its opposing cousin that seeks to dominate the other, does our embeddedness in social life go unacknowledged.

Disregarding the impersonal face of the Other, a human signpost, gives birth to an unacknowledged environment of dismissiveness. While this perspective does not alter the pain, suffering, and anguish of a Holocaust, it points to how such a reality can matriculate upon the human community. In this historical moment, we face another eclipse of the human face. Unlike the Holocaust, which was steeped in overt violence, this moment of precarity often goes undetected within a social space akin to Hannah Arendt's (1963) description of a "banality of evil." Arendt used this phrase to describe the acts of Adolf Eichmann. His bureaucratic involvement in the Holocaust led to the destruction of many. Arendt associates a banality of evil with thoughtlessness, an unwillingness or an inability to comprehend the consequences of one's actions beyond an immediate benefit to self and career.

Precarity orchestrates a social space founded upon ignoring the face of the Other and a banality of evil in which thoughtlessness is a driving social act. The difficulty with events associated with a banality of evil is that they often run beneath the social radar of critique and concern. Indeed, precarity is a banality of evil thriving in this historical moment. Its presence has been announced by multiple scholars, initially by Pierre Bourdieu and most recently by Guy Standing, who acts as a major spokesperson contra precarity.

Shortly before the commencement of the twenty-first century, the notion of precarity became part of our intellectual vocabulary. The primary scholar detailing this form of social destruction was Pierre Bourdieu. Bourdieu defined the notion of the precariat in 1998. His first use of the term was in a collection of essays, primarily composed of political speeches and interviews under the title, *Contre-feux. Propos pour servir à la résistance contre l'invasion néo-libérale* (1998). The English version of this work was *Acts of Resistance: Against the New Myths of Our Time* (1998). Bourdieu repeatedly used the term *précarité*, which when rendered into English stressed the issue of job insecurity. Bourdieu understood precarity as "the erosion of secure and protected employment arrangements" (Schwaller, 2017). More recently, the *Cambridge Encyclopedia of Anthropology* provides a definition of precarity in its 2018 edition. The author of the essay, Sharryn Kasmir, provides a comprehensive and expansive horizon of the use of the term precarity. She acknowledges the term as "a multi-stranded concept" that includes like-related conceptions of labor and life-world insecurity (Kasmir, 2018). Beyond precarity, the terms include precariousness, the precarious, and precaritization. In each case, the terms respond to the excesses of capitalism, dismissive of class differences and, in the vocabulary of this essay, the face of the Other.

The notion of precarity lives in an environment in which organizations and entrepreneurs have shifted risk from the organization and the owners to part-time employees, resulting in use and abuse of the latter. According to Kasmir (2018), Bourdieu's understanding of precarity underscores that "temporary and informal work, in its myriad manifestations, is the predominant mode of livelihood in the late-twentieth to early-twenty-first centuries." Precarity is the result of making part-time workers responsible for risk in an environment inattentive to their voice, concerns, and critical observations. Now, ignoring the precariat is a prediction for political and social unrest (Kasmir, 2018). Bourdieu's original concern has become an ongoing defining threat within the West.

Kasmir's assessment of Bourdieu centers on questions of class, poverty, and the limits of a neoliberal order. Kasmir's (2018) assertion via Bourdieu is that, as one assesses the global economy, only a minority of persons have "secure jobs or steady incomes." Sadly, far too many live through a gig economy or something more akin to barter transactions, to the extent of wading their way through the waste and garbage of others. Precarity announces instability and lack of institutional routine and support that give tomorrow an ongoing linkage with today and the past, rather than each day being an act of uncertainty and survival. The notion of precariousness simply addresses the fact that all socioeconomic groups are unable to control the events before them, whether they be natural disasters, sickness, or historical tragedies. Precariousness, however, is indeed enhanced by class standing and economic background. The biopolitics of precariousness emerge through intensity of recognition that life contains no safety net. Precariousness presupposes that economic, political, and social structures of routine and institutional support are less available to the vulnerable, giving rise to an ongoing sense of hopelessness in a system that seems rigged against one's own success (Kasmir, 2018).

Precarity presupposes ongoing labor uncertainty. Bourdieu (1998) asserts, "Job insecurity is now everywhere" (82). He frames a picture of existence being de-structured. The traditional presupposition of a holistic relationship between "world, time and space" is no longer part of the modern conception of employment and life (Bourdieu, 1998, 82). Granted, such insecurity defines the majority of the world and has long historical roots. The initial hope of modernity and a neoliberal, capitalistic economy was to minimize vulnerability that consistently puts people and families at risk. Those working with capitalistic expectations alone would emphasize the wealth-accumulating ability of such a practical philosophy. The debate on questions of accumulation and its social value guided the chasm between Marxism and the vision of Adam Smith (1723–1790). A neoliberal economy consists of multiple stories: first, the ability to generate goods for people; secondly, the ability to support and nurture institutions for a given culture and society; and thirdly, the most controversial question, the ability of such a practical philosophy to sustain the vulnerable and the economically less privileged.

What distinguishes this historical moment from earlier eras is the commonplace nature of the precariat. The United Kingdom instituted the precariat as part of a checklist on the nature of one's employment. A neoliberal orientation works without an ethic or a soul; it is a machine that takes capital and expands it into more capital. This capital, however, is financial alone. The presupposition of Adam Smith was that social capital would advance simultaneously with economic capital. Such a presupposition is sensible for Smith and his understanding of sympathy. Smith wrote in an era in which sympathy was a social mechanism for understanding and relating to others. As one watched the actions and desires of others, one learned from them. The entire nature of exchange, for Smith, required such learning, with sympathy being the guiding construct for social learning. The obvious question in this contemporary era is, "How did Smith anticipate that sympathy would work, and does it do so today?" Smith assumed that sympathy was the driving force in economic exchange as we learn from one another. His vision was closer to interpersonal bartering than impersonal exploitation of global markets. Today, the discussion centers often on questions of psychological empathy to and for another.

What happens today when observation of and about others seems irrelevant and sympathy is more likely understood as a weak cousin to the notion of empathy? No longer is sympathy understood as a basic mechanism for learning about others. It is closer to a feeling of momentary distress for another that leads to a moral cul-de-sac of inaction. The precariat rests outside the constructive realm of sympathy; its actions and work go ignored and unobserved. The unproductive contemporary understanding of sympathy is more a moment of self-applause for one's concern for the plight of another, which generates no action except, perhaps, a desire to forget such unfavorable feelings causing long-term distress in oneself. The notion of sympathy has shifted from learning to a privileged pause that one seeks to escape, hoping that the duration of the day will not be clouded by such a memory. A neoliberal economy depends upon individualism that fails to recognize pragmatic linkages between and among persons, both the privileged and the vulnerable.

This perspective about the pragmatic reality of addressing precarity centers the work of Guy Standing, who is "a Professorial Research Associate at SOAS University of London and a founding member and honorary co-president of the Basic Income Earth Network (BIEN), a non-governmental organisation that promotes a basic income for all" (Standing, 2021). Standing is perhaps the leading contemporary voice calling into question a neoliberal economic individualism that fails to recognize the long-term social consequences to disparity of wealth and our refusal to take this social moment seriously. His work is a pragmatic call for attention to and for the precariat, both to assist them and to curtail an inevitable social disruption that will transpire with our continued privileged acts of neglect. Standing (2014) states,"The minority is growing by the day. And it is becoming restless, as the millions demonstrating discontent in the squares and parks of great cities testify" (2). Today we find protests in Europe and the United States driven by questions of religious and racial justice. The underlying characteristic in each protest is rebellion against a neoliberal economy that exploits and ignores the vulnerable.

Standing (2011) states that there is an abundance of protests associated with the precariat sentiment. He uses the phrase "primitive rebels" to describe those who are rebelling more against than for (vii). There is an intuitive sense that something is fundamentally wrong with the modern infrastructure of economic distribution. His contention is that primitive protests will eventually mature into sophisticated forms of rebellion. According to Standing, the first stage of any social movement is the development of a common identity. The term "precariat" alone indicates that this first stage is well underway. The second stage, intermingled within the first, is the unleashing of multiple energies tied to a single theme of protest and change. The force of a social moment seldom begins with analytical precision but with an emerging identity and energy. A group of people begin to carve a path that slowly makes sense.

Consider how one might want to construct a sidewalk in a local park. One group might want to engage in a long-term and expensive study about the architectural configuration of where the sidewalk might fit best in the park. Yet, another group, more akin to the raw energy of the precariat, might suggest the following: "Let's examine where people walk. Where are the paths they have already made? Those are the locations for our work and our helping of this park for the people who actually use it." The raw energy of the precariat is carving a path that requires immediate attention and thoughtful pragmatic intervention.

Standing (2014) warns the public that we ignore the precariat at our own peril. He states that the precariat is dangerous because, as predicted in *The Precariat* [2011], the combination of anxiety, alienation, anomie and anger can be expected to lead to more days of riot and protest. And it is dangerous because stress, economic insecurity and frustration can lead and are leading to social illnesses, including drug-taking, petty crime, domestic violence and suicide. (32)

This year of the 2020–21 pandemic has witnessed multiple social protests, which are still somewhat ambiguous but nonetheless in search of clarity of identity and energy that can claim a sense of direction for the abused, the forgotten, and, indeed, the increasingly angry. The following material from *The Guardian* and *The New York Times* offers an impressionistic picture of this energy, born from frustration that acknowledges the inattentiveness of the privileged.

2 An Impressionistic Picture of This Age of Sentiment

In the hope of offering a glimpse of the turbulent sentiment of this precariat moment, I turn to selected essays from *The New York Times* and *The Guardian.* The essays included are description and opinion pieces that render clarity about the nature of the precariat and its socially disturbing sentiment. The following sections provide an impressionistic picture of social experiences creating a precariat sentiment: 1) "Anxiety, Uncertainty, and Stress;" 2) "Physical Risk and Poor Working Conditions;" and 3) "Wage Abuse, Union Busting, and Economic Disparity." The anecdotal accounts comprising this section describe fundamental precariat issues enhanced by the pandemic, suggesting that the virus has placed previously invisible workers within the public eye.

2.1 Anxiety, Uncertainty, and Stress

In The *New York Times*, Hubbard and Donovan (2020) describe the problematic reality of women losing jobs in Beirut and Lebanon, focusing particularly on domestic workers in Saudi Arabia. The authors remind readers of a caustic callousness in which people are laid off with little warning and without wages. Domestic workers discover limited support as other workers, who previously employed them, find their lives moving in problematic economic directions. In the Persian Gulf, there were more than 4 million domestic laborers in 2016. Now, they are laid off, and/or they must suffer reduced wages and problematic working conditions. Hubbard and Donovan (2020) report that "many employers confiscate workers' passports and deprive them of time off…Some prevent them from using cellphones or the internet. Physical and sexual abuse are common." Precarious labor issues were present prior to the pandemic; now they simply augment in severity. For example, a salary of $180 per month is now likely to be cut in half with an increased workload, while employers, under their own stress, become increasingly more hostile. Domestic workers, before the pandemic, already had insufficient time for their own children; this problem is now simply exacerbated. As workers contract the virus, they are abandoned and must go home and put others at risk. For example, an agency in Kenya that recruited a number of domestic workers who contracted the virus refused to respond to any messages or answer the phone. In Saudi Arabia, the task of addressing the safety of workers consumes an inordinate amount of time as one allegation after another reaches public officials.

An essay in *The Guardian* centers on a bus driver, a garbage collector, a fast food worker, a delivery worker, a train driver, and a supermarket worker (Blackall, 2021). The consistency of their stories centers on issues of fear, the difficulty of social distance, and wondering whether or not anyone cares if "I" will live or die. Their fear includes constant anxiety about losing employment, covering for other sick staff, and struggling socially, mentally, and fiscally. In another *Guardian* essay, the focus is on UK supermarket workers who feel forgotten, void of material forms of thankfulness (Pidd and Wolfe-Robinson, 2021). Issues of mask etiquette, long hours, physical risk, and exhaustion generate anger. Staffing shortages require incredibly long hours spent overhearing customers laughing about disobeying social rules of distance in their parties. Not only is the work unappreciated; the work is met with a cavalier spirit of disrespect and disregard that challenges traditional socialization expectations.

Jordan Kisner's (2021) book review of Kayleen Schaefer's *But You're Still So Young: How Thirtysomethings Are Redefining Adulthood* (2021) points to the institutionalizing of a precariat economy. The premise of the book is that the world has changed from the checklist of the 1950s in which one would "finish school, leave home, make your own money, marry and become a parent" (Kisner, 2021); these were ongoing socialization markers that are now called into question. Instead, 30-somethings face financial insecurity, lack of job clarity, rising education costs, and a life driven more by anxiety and stumbling than by previous traditional stages of socialization. Precarity is working its way into families historically supported by clarity and assurance about the future, now part of an uncertain generation.

The New York Times explores the increasingly precarious nature of employment in the pandemic. The essay describes the firing of workers during the pandemic, stating that it takes longer to adapt to unemployment than it does for the death of a loved one (Senior, 2020). Such a statement is extreme, but it does announce the extraordinary pain of economic insecurity. The essay discusses the U.S. Department of Labor reporting more 1.5 million Americans filing for unemployment. Every boss in America must now enact and find training for such difficult conversations. As people are laid off, they need to be assured that there is a procedural sense of fairness in decision making. Without question, such layoffs hurt morale and devastate productivity. The cautionary tale in this historical moment is that good employees are difficult to replace, and the temptation of companies, once those workers are removed, is to place more strain on others in covering jobs previously accomplished by a larger cohort of workers.

This tenuous employment market shapes precariat existence, establishing danger and fear where routine and certainty previously guided action. In addition, the movement of progress tied to capitalism increasingly embraces machines, replacing the labor of individual workers (The Guardian, 2021). This contemporary environment validates a prediction rendered years ago by the late economist Hyman Minsky (1990–1996), who stated that if democracy was to survive the market behavior of the "money manager capitalism," the constant use of algorithms would require active restraint (The Guardian, 2021). The uncertainty of employment includes the increasing inevitability of poor working conditions.

2.2 Physical Risk and Poor Working Conditions

The New York Times reports that dangers for restaurant workers unearth feelings of rage (Wells, 2021). Working in a restaurant asking clients to wear a mask has resulted in altercations while workers are poorly paid and worry for their safety in terms of health and physical protection. The conditions are so severe that employees are asked to sign non-disparagement clauses, curtailing their freedom of speech.

Ginia Bellafante (2020) details how Amazon workers found themselves placed at risk each day during the pandemic. While the Dow Jones Industrial Average stock market index had its worst quarter since 1987, Amazon's stock rose 5%. In her essay, "'We Didn't Sign Up for This': Amazon Workers on the Front Lines," she discusses the necessity of hiring an additional 100,000 workers. She recounts the story of a dissenting worker, Christian Smalls, at a fulfillment center in Staten Island. Smalls contended that the building in which he and his fellow employees labored needed greater attention for sanitation and a strict adherence to protocols related to the virus. For Smalls' efforts, he was fired. Not only did they fire him, they also insulted him in public, stating that he was "not smart or articulate" (Bellafante, 2020). They called his organizing efforts immoral and even, perhaps, illegal. Amazon disputed the fact that he was released because of his acts of agitation, claiming instead that he was released because he came back too quickly during a 14-day paid quarantine in order to lead a demonstration. The mayor of New York required an investigation into Smalls' dismissal, with union leaders and political leaders demanding that Amazon reinstate him. Amazon claims it protects its workers, yet Smalls contended that the facility needed to be shut down long enough for intensive cleaning. While the governor of Kentucky was able to shut down another Amazon fulfillment center long enough for cleaning, in Staten Island the focus remained on testing employees, not sanitizing the facility. During this dispute, Amazon advertised the following: Their workers do "heroic work" (Bellafante, 2020). Yet, the workers persistently view themselves as highly disposable.

The Guardian reports that exploitive working conditions were already a mess pre-pandemic and are now exacerbated (Kelly & Grant, 2020). "Labour and migrant rights groups say that workers in sectors such as furniture, construction, contract cleaning, recycling and domestic work are also being paid less than the minimum wage and experience wage theft, unsafe working conditions, verbal and physical abuse, and unpaid overtime" (Kelly & Grant, 2020). Workers have reported denial of pay, limited wages, poor working conditions, and ongoing abuse. *The Guardian* states that there may be as many as 100,000 people living in conditions of a modern form of slavery in the United Kingdom (Kelly & Grant, 2020).

In an essay entitled, "'We're Modern Slaves': How Meat Plant Workers Became the New Frontline in COVID-19 War," Laughland and Holpuch (2020) discuss COVID-19 deaths at Tyson Foods poultry plants in Georgia. The conditions are simply bleak, with President Trump requiring that such plants remain open and workers risking their own lives by doing their tasks without surgical marks. Without issues of disability and unemployment, the conditions in the meat-packing industry seem little better than the classic depiction in Upton Sinclair's *The Jungle* (1906). In 2020, the working conditions in Chicago's meat-packing industry were horrendous; today's pandemic continues this drama, currently relying primarily on Central American migrants. Another article from *The Guardian* explains that California workers have to choose between continuing employment and protecting their health during the pandemic (Ho, 2020). Workers in the field risk their lives, harvesting produce while simultaneously exposing their lungs to dense smog in the fields. Such conditions require one to risk health while working in the midst of wildfire smoke for $5.50/hour with the addition of $1.60 for every box filled with strawberries.

The Guardian states that the National Health Service (NHS) was urged to not use Personal Protective Equipment (PPE) gloves coming from environments such as Malaysia because they were made under slave-like conditions; the people making the gloves were generally migrants from Bangladesh and Nepal (Pattisson, 2020). "Illegal recruitment fees, long hours, low pay, passport confiscation and squalid, overcrowded accommodation are commonplace, workers have claimed. Experts say such conditions leave them vulnerable to forced labour and debt bondage, which are modern forms of slavery" (Pattisson, 2020). The United Kingdom called this situation modern slavery in a document, "UK Government Modern Slavery Statement," published in March 2020 (Manzoni, 2020). This particular production of healthcare equipment was fraught with difficulties; *The Guardian* investigated two large suppliers of medical gloves and found multiple indicators of passport confiscation, forced overtime, and wages withheld (Pattisson, 2020).

In addition to the problematic conditions discussed above, healthcare professionals meet similar reactions from their employers, permitting their health and financial wellbeing to decline (Lee, 2020). In a private online document, more than 1200 workers shared their stories, which pointed to their pandemic work as akin to warzone employment. The comment from one professional was that CDC protocols were changing so rapidly that people were simply scared to get up in the morning and go to work. It seems that no profession can escape the neoliberal movement toward the maximization of profit, moving risk from institution to employee.

Not only are workers placed in precarious health and employment positions, their actions are increasingly investigated. For example, *The New York Times* reports increased surveillance during the pandemic as numerous people work at home (Satariano, 2020). Employers scrutinize time utilization, prompting a greater investment in monitoring software. The goal is to maintain productivity, but the byproduct is a "creepy" form of surveillance (Satariano, 2020). Adam Satariano explored the software, securing it for himself and engaging in his own self-surveillance. He offers an autoethnographic account of his experience with "employee-monitoring software made by Hubstaff, an Indianapolis company." Satariano gave control of this software to his editor. After three weeks of monitoring, he and his editor collectively offered the following intellectual assessment: "Ick." The software costs the user about $7–20 a month. Workers know they are being watched and that privacy is increasingly violated. The software marks information at 10-min intervals with a productivity score. The software mapped usage of his social media sites, including Twitter and Spotify, as well as when he was hunting for food and going on bicycle trips. The software knew his GPS coordinates, following him during jogs and wine shopping. The software even had closeups of his Google conference calls. The result was that Satariano's productivity was listed at 45%. Satariano states that a marketing company with which he consulted permitted employees to work from home and immediately found a drop in productivity and in sales. Such companies are intrigued by such software as they struggle for increased productivity. Interestingly, while engaging the software, Satariano found ways to cheat, enhancing a public record of his account of "productivity." Rebellion emerges from such surveillance and lack of trust. All of us know people that do extraordinarily good work in short periods of time and others who require much longer periods of time to complete a lesser quality of work. This software rewards the latter, not the former. Hearkening back to a book by James Buchan called *Crowded with Genius: The Scottish Enlightenment: Edinburgh's Moment of the Mind* (2004), it appears that the legacy of the surveillance software is to make sure that the internet space will not be "crowded with genius" but rather with those who plod consistently through the day. Perhaps in this historical moment only those in control consider themselves geniuses, at least until someone else attempts to control them. This historical moment finds definition in professional abuse.

2.3 Wage Abuse, Union Busting, and Economic Disparity

Workers poorly paid found themselves without compensation as their employers refused payment (Scheiber, 2020). Employees in a variety of areas of the economy, from domestic work to construction to food preparation, experience not only unemployment but also reduction in their already low wages. When the market is difficult and jobs are few, public complaints from employees go unattended. The following quote from Angeles Solis, the "lead organizer for Make the Road New York, a group that promotes the interests of immigrant workers," indicates the nature of the concern: "Wage theft and a myriad of labor abuses have increased during the pandemic, and they've increased on an already vulnerable population" (Scheiber, 2020). Scaling back hours and wages during the pandemic creates a perfect storm for those least protected. Employers want minimal enforcement of labor considerations during times of heightened panic. Contrarily, the argument of workers is that, during such moments, labor and wage standards must be aggressively supported.

The distribution of wealth is now part of public conversation. Adler and Schneider (2020) examine the disparity between Amazon's then CEO, Jeff Bezos, whose personal wealth advanced by $10 billion in a single day during the pandemic, and the financial uncertainty of warehouse laborers. With an Amazon fulfillment center in Poznań, Poland, a strike called for greater paid protection. The pandemic has announced an incredible inequity in wealth, with a typical Amazon worker on the warehouse floor making approximately $30,000 per year and Bezos, again, making $10 billion in a day.

Exploited workers in a UK garment factory stated that more than £27 million was stolen from them as they were systematically underpaid (Davies, 2020). The concerns of the workers were not taken seriously as wages went into the hands of administrators, managers, and owners of production. Exploiting vulnerable workers and robbing them of tens of millions of pounds, in an environment of limited safety conditions and poor health and clearly lack of concern, seems increasingly commonplace.

The pandemic did not create economic inequality but exacerbated it, unmasking the reality of indifference to labor justice (Smialek, 2020). Only the top 10% of investors found themselves wealthier in 2019 than they did prior to the Great Recession of 2007–09. 94% of the wealthiest families are stock-heavy, benefiting during the pandemic, whereas only 1 out of 5 poorer families are invested in the market. As those at the bottom of the economic scale began to catch up from the economic events of 2007–09, the pandemic altered all hope. Issues of race are evident; in 2019, Black families had 15% less net wealth than white families—approximately \$24,100 for Black families and \$36,100 for Hispanic families in comparison to \$188,200 for white families. The differences are even starker when considering inherited wealth. For example, the wealthiest 1% in 2019 would have an inheritance of \$1.6 million, while those at the bottom of the economic food chain would inherit an average of \$30,000. Not only is there disparity in the current financial environment, but also wealth transmission makes the future bleak. Robert Gebeloff (2021) continues conversation about disparity in wealth tied to class and race, reporting that 30 years ago in the United States the top 5% controlled half of the nation's wealth, whereas today they control two-thirds. Such conditions fuel momentum for labor reform and unionization.

One example of laborers attempting to protect themselves comes from Cort Furniture Rental in New Jersey (Silver-Greenberg & Abrams, 2020). They attempted to unionize. The company, owned by Warren Buffett's Berkshire Hathaway Inc., replaced truck drivers with subcontractors, which stopped the plans for union organizing. Companies indicate that layoffs are necessary in difficult economic conditions, with corporate critics suggesting that workers are often punished in order to discourage unionization. Neoliberal critics suggest a pattern in the American business landscape, continued by the pandemic: protecting the company and minimizing labor solidarity. Joseph A. McCartin, a labor historian at Georgetown University, examined the ways in which the 1918 pandemic, this pandemic, and other events such as the Great Depression resulted in the targeting of union activity. Such actions included "union busting" and increasing disparity between managers and their laboring counterparts (Silver-Greenberg & Abrams, 2020). The contrast in wealth accumulation in the modern workplace is far from fiction: During 1947–79, the ration of wages from top to lowest earner was 3.18-to-1. In 2018, it was 6.04-to-1 (Mishel & Kandra, 2020). Again, the call for solidarity of labor has a background of fact.

Adam Witt, at a Jersey Shore University Medical Center, took a day off to help defend and support a nurse whose presence was required at a disciplinary hearing (Scheiber & Rosenthal, 2020). He was the union president of the local nurses. His action resulted in his firing. With similar outcomes, Scheiber and Rosenthal (2020) state that during the coronavirus a large number of people have clashed with employers. The companies have not protected or valued their labor. The scope of this dismissive drama includes grocery workers, flight attendants, warehouse workers, and healthcare workers, among others. The implications of this impressionistic picture of the precariat dwell more within repetition than uniqueness of historical moment.

Implications: Déjà Vu

Since Bourdieu, multiple scholars have contributed to his insights. In an essay written for *The Guardian* 23 years after Bourdieu first used the term "precariat," Julian Coman (2021) suggests that the world is at a fulcrum point of division, nurturing the possibility of global revolution. To substantiate his case, Coman provides an interpretive picture of Paris commemorating the 150th anniversary of Paris Commune's vision of radical democracy. His essay reminds us that Paris is and has been a place of labor awakening.

The Commune movement of 1871 was anarchic, supported by the poor and hated by three different groups: the monarchists, the conservatives, and the liberal bourgeoise. Richard Nelsson (2019) states that the communards were "a radical, popular led government that ruled Paris from 18 March to 28 May, 1871." They arose in the wake of France's Franco-German war defeat and "the collapse of Napoleon III's Second Empire (1852–70)," overthrowing the French regime that failed during the Prussian siege (Nelsson, 2019). The communards had a practical agenda; they wanted their representatives to be accountable, for women to have a vote, for there to be equal pay, and for homes to be found for the homeless. The Commune called for citizenship for foreigners and access of all to and under the law. After commanding control of Paris, "the elected council of the Commune passed socialist policies and oversaw city functions" (Nelsson, 2019). They were met with vicious suppression via the French army, and were eventually overthrown. Coman (2021) notes that this event generated wounds that are yet to heal.

During that bloody week of the 21st–28th of May 1871, between 8000 and 20,000 communards lost their lives at barricades or by firing squads. Violence seemed to spiral out of control. During this time, the Archbishop and more than 50 other hostages, many of them being priests, were killed by communards. The moment seemed to be a revolutionary experiment, pointing to the necessity of future generations taking communism seriously. "Karl Marx described the Commune as the 'glorious harbinger of a new society.' Lenin saw it as the forerunner to the Russian revolution" (Coman, 2021). In the beginning days of fascism and foreshadowing World War II, France had a popular front government centered on anti-fascism. In 1936, that government witnessed more than 500,000 make a pilgrimage to the Père Lachaise cemetery with the objective of honoring the martyrs of the Commune, whose names are written on the Mur des Fédérés, or Communards' Wall. There, "the last of the Communard insurgents, cornered by government forces, fought a hopeless, all-night battle among the tombstones. In the morning, the 147 survivors were lined up against this completely ordinary, plain brick wall, shot, and buried where they fell in a mass grave" (Paris, 2015).

Coman (2021) comments that "there are lots of echoes with today;" 1871 demonstrated great division, which continued in the pilgrimage of 1936 and the student protests of 1968, echoing within the precariat protests of today.

In France, the events of July 14, 1879, now known as Bastille Day, seem woven into the collective national memory. Yet, the events of 1871 are largely ignored. People considered the 1871 protests beyond the norm of respectable life, but today memory of the communards is once again dividing Paris. The Communard commemoration events began on March 18, 2021. The mayor of Paris, Anne Hidalgo, planted a tree at Montmartre (Vock, 2021), the heart of this revolt and repression, and "inaugurated a programme of 50 events commemorating the Commune, including exhibitions, plays, conferences and debates" (AFP, 2021). Additionally, Place Louise Michel, which carries the namesake of the most famous communard, once again found parishioners filling the space and carrying silhouettes of shoemakers, washerwomen, and bakers who tried to garner control of the capital in 1871. The commemoration, aptly named Nous La Commune (We the Commune), consisted of educational, musical, and poetic renderings of the power of that time and space.

As one might expect in this historical moment of fragmentation and division, not all met this moment of celebration with enthusiasm. Opposing reactions have emerged, with historian Mathilde Larrere commenting that "the memory of the Commune remains deeply divisive," making it seem "as if we were back in 1871" (AFP, 2021). While officials in Paris assisted with the commemorative moment, stating that in 1871 these were revolutionaries and today they should be better understood as "radical pioneers" (Coman, 2021), protestors have gathered on the steps of Sacré-Coeur. Some have suggested that the commemoration is a celebration of ideology and bloodshed, with some accusing Hidalgo of attempting to secure support from the Left in preparation for next year's presidential election. Conservatives have repeatedly objected to any subsidies given to the friends of the Commune, who are organizing and, in the words of some, glorifying those violent events. Le Monde talked about the tense nature of this anniversary and L'Express even asked the question if it should be celebrated (Coman, 2021). In a time of increasing fragmentation, no clear, straight answer is universally available.

The reason for the obvious renewal of interest in the communards is that the poor of then are the poor of now. More than 150 years later, the "poorly paid precariat is voicing similar demands" (Coman, 2021). The communards comprise the public memory of the struggle of what is now termed the precariat. This impressionistic picture of contemporary inequities of labor and wealth, witnessed through a variety of descriptive, opinion-driven essays about events in the United States and Europe, announces the reality of Guy Standing's warning that we must take the protests tied to precariat concerns seriously. To fail to do so puts much at risk.

Returning to Emmanuel Levinas, he claimed that the task of the human being is to attend to ethics as first philosophy. This is only possible when the face of the Other claims our responsible attention. Otherwise, we invite ongoing disparity to the point of instigating revolution. Working with Guy Standing's title of *The Precariat* (2011), perhaps a Levinasian subtitle is meaningful: The Forgotten Face, an Awakened Revolution. Levinas provides no answers for a template inviting a perfect world. He simply reminds us that we have a fundamental obligation to ethics. Prior to ontology, prior to Being, there is an ethical call: "I am my brother's keeper." When we ignore such a call, we do so at our own peril. We are social creatures, derivatively created by our environments and others. It is unexamined acts of privilege that permit some people to ignore our phenomenological connection to one another. This era is a bumbling malaise of dissatisfaction.

Levinas repeatedly states that a derivative creature responsible for the Other ultimately engages life with the following mantra: "I am my brother's keeper." The shadow side of this statement lurks in the alleys of dismissive inattention to anyone but "me" and "my kind." Today, however, one protest after another, surrounding gender, race, affectivity, and economic disparity, is calling the human community to attend to an immemorial call of responsibility for the Other. The notion of the precariat is not simply an example of fiscal inequality; it is a call to respond to the human face and our obligation to one another. Levinas (1968/1998) often used the phrase "otherwise than Being." In this historical moment, it is "otherwise than inattentiveness."

References

Adler, D., & Schneider, J. (2020, December 1). Amazon workers are fighting for their rights. This holiday season, think of them. *The Guardian*. https://www.theguardian.com/commentisfree/2020/dec/01/amazon-workers-fighting-for-their-rights. Accessed 21 April 2021.

AFP. (2021, March 23). Commemoration begins of the bloody weeks of the Paris Commune of 1871. *The Local*. https://www.thelocal.fr/20210323/commemoration-begins-of-the-bloody-weeks-of-the-paris-commune-of-1871/. Accessed 26 April 2021.

Arendt, H. (1963). *Eichmann in Jerusalem: A report on the banality of evil*. Viking Press.

Bellafante, G. (2020, April 3). 'We didn't sign up for this': Amazon workers on the front lines. *The New York Times*. https://www.nytimes.com/2020/04/03/nyregion/coronavirus-nyc-chris-smalls-amazon.html. Accessed 15 April 2021.

Blackall, M. (2021, February 8). 'We get daily abuse': UK frontline workers on the COVID second wave. *The Guardian*. https://www.theguardian.com/world/2021/feb/08/we-get-daily-abuse-uk-frontline-workers-on-the-covid-second-wave. Accessed 21 April 2020.

Bourdieu, P. (1998). *Acts of resistance: Against the new myths of our time*. Polity.

Coman, J. (2021, March 7). Vive la Commune? The working-class insurrection that shook the world. *The Guardian*. https://www.theguardian.com/world/2021/mar/07/vive-la-commune-the-working-class-insurrection-that-shook-the-world. Accessed 27 May 2021.

Davies, R. (2020, October 11). Exploited workers at UK garment factories 'robbed' of £27m since July. *The Guardian*. https://www.theguardian.com/business/2020/oct/11/exploited-workers-at-uk-garment-factories-robbed-of-27m-since-july. Accessed 22 April 2021.

Gebeloff, R. (2021, January 16). Who owns stocks? Explaining the rise in inequality during the pandemic. *The New York Times*. https://www.nytimes.com/2021/01/26/upshot/stocks-pandemic-inequality.html?searchResultPosition=9. Accessed 26 April 2021.

The Guardian. (2021, March 21). *The Guardian view on finance failures: Manmade errors amplified by machines*. https://www.theguardian.com/commentisfree/2021/mar/21/the-guardian-view-on-finance-failures-manmade-errors-amplified-by-machines. Accessed 23 April 2021.

Ho, V. (2020, August 23). 'An impossible choice': Farmworkers pick a paycheck over health despite smoke-filled air. *The Guardian*. https://www.theguardian.com/us-news/2020/aug/22/california-farmworkers-wildfires-air-quality-coronavirus. Accessed 22 April 2021.

Hubbard, B., & Donovan, L. (2020, July 6). Laid off and locked up: Virus traps domestic workers in Arab states. *The New York Times*. https://www.nytimes.com/2020/07/06/world/middleeast/coronavirus-saudi-domestic-workers-maids-arab.html. Accessed 26 April 2021.

Indeed. (2021). *Amazon.com warehouse worker yearly salaries in the united states*. https://www.indeed.com/cmp/Amazon.com/salaries/Warehouse-Worker#:~:text=How%20much%20does%20a%20Warehouse,which%20meets%20the%20national%20average. Accessed 27 May 2021.

Kasmir, S. (2018). Precarity. In F. Stein et al. (Hrsg.), *The Cambridge encyclopedia of anthropology*. https://www.anthroencyclopedia.com/entry/precarity. Accessed 27 May 2021.

Kelly, A., & Grant, H. (2020, July 17). Labour abuses happening 'at scale' far beyond Leicester, warn rights groups. *The Guardian*. https://www.theguardian.com/global-development/2020/jul/17/nobody-holds-them-to-account-labour-abuses-go-far-beyond-leicester. Accessed 21 April 2021.

Kisner, J. (2021, March 3). The panic of the 30-somethings, and more. *The New York Times*. https://www.nytimes.com/2021/03/03/books/review/but-youre-still-so-young-kayleen-schaefer-spilt-milk-courtney-zoffness-randa-jarrar-love-is-an-ex-country.html. Accessed 26 April 2021.

Laughland, O., & Holpuch, A. (2020, May 2). 'We're modern slaves': How meat plant workers became the new frontline in Covid-19 war. *The Guardian*. https://www.theguardian.com/world/2020/may/02/meat-plant-workers-us-coronavirus-war. Accessed 21 April 2021.

Lee, E. (2020, March 25). Nurses share coronavirus stories anonymously in an online document. *The New York Times*. https://www.nytimes.com/2020/03/25/business/media/coronavirus-nurses-stories-anonymous.html. Accessed 21 April 2021.

Levinas, E. (1968/1998). *Otherwise than being*. Trans. A. Lingis. Duquesne University Press.

Manzoni, J. (2020, March 18). UK government modern slavery statement. *Gov.UK*. https://assets.publishing.service.gov.uk/government/uploads/system/uploads/attachment_data/file/875800/UK_Government_Modern_Slavery_Statement.pdf. Accessed 26 April 2021.

Mishel, L., & Kandra, J. (2020, August 18). CEO compensation surged 14% in 2019 to $21.3 million. *Economic Policy Institute*. https://www.epi.org/publication/ceo-compensation-surged-14-in-2019-to-21-3-million-ceos-now-earn-320-times-as-much-as-a-typical-worker/#:~:text=CEO%20compensation%20in%202018%20(the,over%20the%201947%E2%80%931979%20period. Accessed 26 April 2021.

Nelsson, R. (2019, June 26). The Paris Commune—From the archive, 1871. *The Guardian*. https://www.theguardian.com/world/from-the-archive-blog/2019/jun/26/the-paris-commune-from-the-archive-1871. Accessed 27 May 2021.

Paris. (2015). *Cimetière du Père Lachaise*. https://en.parisinfo.com/paris-museum-monument/71470/Cimetiere-du-Pere-Lachaise. Accessed 27 May 2021.

Parker, K., et al. (2020, December 9). How the Coronavirus outbreak has—and hasn't—changed the way Americans work. *Pew Research Center*. https://www.pewresearch.org/social-trends/2020/12/09/how-the-coronavirus-outbreak-has-and-hasnt-changed-the-way-americans-work/. Accessed 26 April 2021.

Pattisson, P. (2020, April 23). NHS urged to avoid PPE gloves made in 'slave-like' conditions. *The Guardian*. https://www.theguardian.com/global-development/2020/apr/23/nhs-urged-to-avoid-ppe-gloves-made-in-slave-like-conditions-coronavirus. Accessed 22 April 2021.

Pidd, H., & Wolfe-Robinson, M. (2021, January 10). UK supermarket staff say they have become the 'forgotten key workers.' *The Guardian*. https://www.theguardian.com/business/2021/jan/10/uk-supermarket-staff-say-they-have-become-the-forgotten-key-workers. Accessed 22 April 2021.

Satariano, A. (2020, May 6). How my boss monitors me while I work from home. *The New York Times*. https://www.nytimes.com/2020/05/06/technology/employee-monitoring-work-from-home-virus.html. Accessed 16 April 2020.

Scheiber, N. (2020, September 3). Stiffing workers on wages grows worse with recession. *The New York Times*. https://www.nytimes.com/2020/09/03/business/economy/wage-theft-recession.html. Accessed 15 April 2021.

Scheiber, N., & Rosenthal, B. M. (2020, April 9). Nurses and doctors speaking out on safety now risk their job. *The New York Times*. https://www.nytimes.com/2020/04/09/business/coronavirus-health-workers-speak-out.html. Accessed 21 April 2021.

Schwaller, C. (2017, December 15). *#Precarity everywhere. Allegra Lab: Anthropology for Radical Optimism*. https://allegralaboratory.net/precarity-everywhere/. Accessed 20 May 2021.

Senior, J. (2020, June 14). More people will be fired in the pandemic. Let's talk about it. *The New York Times*. https://www.nytimes.com/2020/06/14/opinion/layoffs-coronavirus-economy.html. Accessed 26 April 2021.

Silver-Greenberg, J., & Abrams, R. (2020, April 28). Fired in a pandemic 'because we tried to start a union,' workers say. *The New York Times*. https://www.nytimes.com/2020/04/28/business/coronavirus-unions-layoffs.html. Accessed 15 April 2021.

Smialek, J. (2020, September 28). Even as Americans grew richer, inequality persisted. *The New York Times*. https://www.nytimes.com/2020/09/28/business/economy/coronavirus-pandemic-income-inequality.html. Accessed 23 April 2021.

Standing, G. (2011). *The precariat: The new dangerous class.* Bloomsbury Academic.
Standing, G. (2014). *A precariat charter: From denizens to citizens.* Bloomsbury Academic.
Standing, G. (2021). https://www.guystanding.com/. Accessed 27 May 2021.
Wells, P. (2021, January 5). From toxic chefs to COVID, restaurant workers deserve better. *The New York Times.* https://www.nytimes.com/2021/01/05/dining/restaurant-workers-ndas-david-chang.html. Accessed 15 April 2020.
Vock, I. (2021, March 18). After 150 years, the legacy of the Paris Commune continues to divide France. *New Statesman.* https://www.newstatesman.com/world/europe/2021/03/after-150-years-legacy-paris-commune-continues-divide-france. Accessed 27 May 2021.

Pandemic and Control Society

Rolf Dieter Hepp

Out of this crisis, new techniques of leadership are intensifying. Discipline and norms are no longer suitable enough to ensure productivity in today's world, which is why there is a shift towards self-directed processes and mechanisms such as flexibility, motivation and goal setting. The actors are therefore no longer assigned a fixed place in the sense of discipline, but are encouraged to surrender to the new control mechanisms and to adapt themselves again and again with a high degree of self-control. The realistic fear of contagion reinforces the actors' willingness to submit to these forms of mobilization.

According to official sources, the social, political and economic crisis that posed existential threats to health and the economy worldwide began in China in the winter of 2019.

A previously unknown lung disease emerged, which soon proved to be highly contagious and often life-threatening. The first death occurred as early as January 11, 2020. It went from a local endemic to a worldwide pandemic in no time. On January 27, various German media first reported a case of infection in Germany, in Starnberg, Bavaria. Since then, over 91,300 people have died from the disease in Germany alone up to and including August 2021 (DESTATIS, 2021). As of February 11, 2020, the World Health Organization calls it "Covid-19". Globally, not only did the economy begin to tumble, but the social contexts of life in the

R. D. Hepp (✉)
Freie Universität Berlin, Berlin, Germany
e-mail: falsekerghepp@gmx.de

R. D. Hepp (ed.), *Shifts and Reorientation Within the Social-Crisis and Catastrophe: Towards the Realization of Pandemic Epistemological Processes*, Prekarisierung und soziale Entkopplung – transdisziplinäre Studien,
https://doi.org/10.1007/978-3-658-43041-2_8

developed parts of the world, such as Europe and the United States, were also incisively affected.

In Germany, too, the impact was immense. "The Corona pandemic and the measures used to combat it triggered the most severe recession in German post-war history" (Bonin et al., 2020, p. 13). The number of unemployed in Germany increased by 19.59 percent within one year from January 2020 to January 2021, from 2,425,523 to 2,900,663 people looking for work. Even more dramatic was the 851 percent increase in people on short-time work during the same period, from 382,423 to 3,636,911, meaning that in January 2021, 2,244,063 people in Germany were unemployed or threatened with unemployment (Federal Statistical Office (ed.), 2021). This means that around 12 percent of all people of working age between 16 and 65 in Germany were unemployed or threatened with unemployment. In addition, wage levels also declined as a result of the pandemic (Federal Ministry for Economic Affairs and Energy, 2021, p. 114 f).

However, this did not affect all people in Germany to the same extent. In the short term, it mainly affected people with lower labor market integration in the hospitality industry and simple and household-related services (Bonin et al., 2020, p. 19). Artists are just as much a part of the vulnerable segment of society that had their income taken away by the lockdown. With the Lockdown 2020, the status of art and culture in society is readjusted;- art is equated with the leisure sector and the entertainment industry instead of being assigned to the educational and development potential of the actors. The accompanying devaluation of the role of art in society increases the vulnerability of the artists concerned and thus creates new lines of conflict and new potential for social conflict.

Since the risk of job loss was particularly high for the self-employed, they were the most likely, along with semi-skilled workers and people with an immigrant background, to be forced to accept a drop in their standard of living and to use reserves. Households with five or more persons, younger households and single parents were most likely to experience financial difficulties. In summary, the Corona pandemic threatens to exacerbate the financial situation of disadvantaged groups.

In this context, fear for one's own life or the life of a loved one was a crucial means to get the population behind the state and the direction taken to avert the danger. Thus, according to representative surveys, the government's Corona policy received a high level of approval among large segments of the population. Particularly among those citizens whose sense of fear was relatively high, the politicians who took a pioneering role in their demands and implementation of more stringent measures were especially popular. In a threat situation, the unknown itself was "uncanny" to the actors (cf. Freud (1919) on the uncanny).

Politicians, who are responsible for decisions and directions to be taken, are also not immune to such fears. At the beginning of the pandemic, the unknown virus and the images from Bergamont created a threat environment in which the government (possibly itself frightened) had to do everything in its power to protect the population. Communicating threats, insecurities, and fears to the population at large should presumably adjust the population's behavior to the threat environment. A look at countries where governments did not take the danger of the virus seriously or even downplayed it shows how devastating this was for thousands and thousands of lives and countless after-effects of the disease.

At the same time, the fear of health threats within our society was only intensified by government action. The decision to take ever more drastic measures and the communication about them led to the collective perception of being in a real and acute threat situation. In statements to the population, the protection of life and health was seen as the goal and legitimation of these measures. Fears were at least perpetuated through televised speeches by the German Chancellor, announcements by the Robert Koch Institute and expert interviews in the print media and on television. Such fears, such as the fear of suffocation or of the powerlessness of relatives, led to an understanding of and support for the measures among a broad majority of society. In addition to the important implementation of hygiene behavior rules, however, actions such as hamster purchases of certain products also testified to the fear that drove many actors. Here, too, the statistics hit home: the daily announcement of incidence figures continues to control the level of fear to this day. The higher the numbers, the higher the level of fear in society.

A collective feeling of fear can act as a motivator to bring about the implementation of behavioral changes within a society. On the other hand, this fear can also take on a life of its own and cause reactions in the population that were not planned or intended. An example of this is the increasing disenchantment with politics among the population, which seems to be spreading more and more. Black pedagogy also worked with feelings of guilt. Parents blamed their children for their parents' bad moods or for other negative family situations. Today, the evocation of feelings of guilt, through public statements by politicians, causes actors who do not want to comply with constraints to feel guilty and thus mutate into addressees of exclusion. Conversely, it can be said that when these people comply with the conditions, it is sometimes out of the motivation of not wanting to feel guilty. This can be interpreted as a subtle form of intimidation that has its roots in black pedagogy. Mutual recriminations also grow out of this.

Another fear is the fear of political-social restrictions;- of a further lockdown and the immense cuts in the working and living environment of many social groups and, individuals that will come with it.... Parents, children, young people, restaurateurs, retailers, cultural workers, etc.; they all experience an additional burden on a financial, psychological and social level, up to an uncanny form of existential fear.

Corona carries something sinister into society. One cannot sensually perceive the danger, since aerosols and droplet infections cannot be tasted, smelled, or felt. When such modes of transmission first appeared in medical literature in the nineteenth century, they were discounted as speculation and rejected because they did not meet accepted scientific criteria.

"In the seventeenth and eighteenth centuries, the idea gained ground that contagions in certain diseases occur through a contagium vitum, a substance invisible to the eye, which is transmitted from one person to another. However, in the absence of observation of microorganisms, this notion remained unproven and contestable. Just as the most advanced physicians were applying stricter scientific standards in the 1800s, the idea of contagion through human contact was discredited. (...). It was precisely the proponents of a strictly scientific method who denied the existence of contagium vitum and rejected the doctrine of "contagionism," according to which contagion occurs through contact, as an outmoded error, an "absurd hypothesis," a "remnant of childish ideas": for who would ever have perceived these mysterious diseases? (Goudsblom, 1979, p. 229, translation by Rolf Hepp)

Today, the population is also seen as a potential carrier and transmitter of the viruses and bacteria precisely because of aerosols during the pandemic. Through such forms of subjectivization of the viral problem, the actors are identified as carriers of the pandemic events.

In anchoring such views in social discourses, a tried and tested "neoliberal" tradition of dismantling social security systems is taken up and at the same time reinforced by fears and feelings of guilt in order to achieve an orientation of the population toward the restrictions on the potential for action during the pandemic, since measures such as lockdowns and/or restrictions on freedom must be accepted as necessary by the actors.

Fears and feelings of guilt are mobilized for this purpose. Targeted or untargeted confusion is promoted by a systematic production of uncertainty, which on the one hand plays with the fears, anxieties and hopes of the actors, but on the other hand tries to channel and orient them towards an attitude of acceptance of the "necessary" subjugation strategies to fight the virus.

Debt does not only mean economy but at the same time involves a whole arsenal of security techniques, calculations, measurements and an establishment of equivalences through which the entire existence of the debtor is shaped. Thus, the debt situation does not only refer to the present, but involves coordinations, conditionings and orientations to the future life contexts of the creditor, as well as the debtor.

"In the light of the neoliberal debt economy, the Second Essay of the Genealogy takes on a new topicality: debt is not only an economic mechanism, it is also a security-state technique of government aimed at reducing the uncertainty of the behavior of the governed. By training the governed to "promise" (to honor their debt), capitalism exercises "control over the future," since debt obligations allow one to foresee, calculate, measure,and establish equivalences between current and future behavior. The effects ofthe power of debt on subjectivity (guilt and responsibility) allow capitalism to bridge the gap between present and future." Lazzaratto, p.45)

Since debts create a bond, a relationship between the present and the future, between creditor and debtor at the same time, the disposal of the future flows into the network of relationships as a "social fact" in Durkheim's sense, or determines and arranges the roles at the two poles of the oppositional relationship creditor/debtor. Thus, the future is immediately structured, objectified and subjectified by sorting it into the corresponding chains of action.

"The debt economy is an economy of time and subjectivation in a specific sense. Indeed, neo liberalism is an economy turned toward the future, since finance is a promise of future wealth and, consequently, incommensurable with actual wealm. No use making a fuss because the economy's "present" and "future" fail to match up! What matters is finance's goal of reducing what will be to what is, that is, reducing the future and it possibilities to current power relations. From this perspective, all financial innovations have one sole purpose: possessing the future in advance by objectivizing it. This objectivation is of a completely different order from mat of labor time; objectivizing time, possessing it in advance, means subordinating all possibility of choice and decision which the future holds to the reproduction of capitalist power relations. In this way, debt appropriates not only the present labor time of wage-earners and of me population in general, it also preempts non-chronological time, each person's future as well as the future of society as a whole. The principal explanation for the strange sensation of living in a society without time, without possibility, without foreseeable rupture, is debt." (Lazzarato, 2012, 55 f.)

The dismantling of security systems produces an insecure world that carries indeterminacy within itself and is tailored to precarious life contexts. Corona Bekämpfung ties in with these tendencies in order to be able to develop mobilization potentials Indeterminacy is a permanent crossroads;- in which decisions are based on poverty.

During the pandemic, seemingly all political and social actions and activities focus on fighting the pandemic. Pandemic control is the focus of political and public interest. To this end, the population must be mobilized to support díe measures and restrictions. Ernst Jünger considers mobilization to be a formative factor of modernity that structures, orders and aligns individuals. This refers not only to mobilization for World War I, but also determines the fate of the worker and the clerk, who are encouraged to move constantly. (Compare Jünger, 2013, Der Arbeiter (The Worker)). According to Agamben, the state of exception that is sought with the mobilization of the masses is described as authoritarian rule, following and echoing Foucault. "Sovereign is who decides on the state of exception". (Schmitt, 2021, p. 13)

Whoever can determine the state of emergency is the sovereign. As early as 1899, Thorstein Veblen pointed out in the "Theory of the Leisure Class" that the existing society, although peaceful, was built on a war-oriented system based on subjugation.

"During the predatory stage proper the distinction between the leisure and the labouring class is in some degree a ceremonial distinction only. The able bodied men jealously stand aloof from whatever is in their apprehension, menial drudgery; but their activity in fact contributes appreciably to the sustenance of the group. The subsequent stage of quasi-peaceable industry is usually characterised by an established chattel slavery, herds of cattle, and a servile class of herdsmen and shepherds; industry has advanced so far that the community is no longer dependent for its livelihood on the chase or on any other form of activity that can fairly be classed as exploit. From this point on, the characteristic feature of leisure class life is a conspicuous exemption from all useful employment. The normal and characteristic occupations of the class in this mature phase of its life history are in form very much the same as in its earlier days. These occupations are government, war, sports, and devout observances. Persons unduly given to difficult theoretical niceties may hold that these occupations are still incidentally and indirectly "productive"; but it is to be noted as decisive of the question in hand that the ordinary and ostensible motive of the leisure class in engaging in these occupations is assuredly not an increase of wealth by productive effort. At this as at any other cultural stage, government and war are, at least in part, carried on for the pecuniary gain of those who engage in them; but it is gain obtained by the honourable method of seizure and conversion. These occupations are of the nature of predatory, not of productive, employment. Something similar may be said of the chase, but with a difference. As the community passes out of the hunting stage proper, hunting gradually becomes differentiated into two distinct employments. On the one hand it is a trade, carried on chiefly for gain; and from this the element of exploit is virtually absent, or it is at any rate not present in a sufficient degree to clear the pursuit of the imputation of gainful industry. On the other hand, the chase is also a sport—an exercise of the predatory impulse simply. As such it does not afford any appreciable pecuniary incentive, but it contains a more or less obvious element of exploit. It is this latter development of the chase—purged of all imputation of handicraft—thatalone is meritorious and fairly belongs in the scheme of life of the developed leisure class." (Veblen, 1899, p. 20)

According to Foucault, the plague forms an ideal model as a "dream of the order politicians", All actors are fixed in one place, controlled and monitored. The panoptic principle of organization provides a model of control and surveillance of individuals, so that disciplining produces subjects. Today, according to Deleuze, through mechanisms of the society of control, individual subjects are no longer monitored in a specific place; instead, the methods of surveillance are carried forward by gaining an overview of the movement of actors through fluctuations, which experience an inherent weight and amplification in the pandemic as a real existing threat scenario.

Power, and thus profit, is no longer necessarily gained from disciplining the individual body, but by directing and controlling movements and flows.

According to Deleuze, the society of control unfolds primarily through the control of movements, the legibility of bodies and data streams, and the modulation of individuals. Thus, individuals are not fixed and enclosed in single closed institutions but, on the contrary, individuals are kept in constant movement and flexibility. The body is no longer adapted to the large machinery, but is constantly "modulated".

"The disciplinary societies have two poles: the signature that designates the individual, and the number or administrative numeration that indicates his or her position within a mass. This is because the disciplines never saw any incompatibility between these two, and because at the same time power individualizes and masses together, that is, constitutes those over whom it exercises power into a body and molds the individuality of each member of that body. (Foucault saw the origin of this double charge in the pastoral power of the priest—the flock and each of its animals–but civil power moves in turn and by other means to make itself lay "priest".) In the societies of control, on the other hand, what is important is no longer either a signature or a number, but a code: the code is a password, while on the other hand disciplinary societies are regulated by watchwords (as much from the point of view of integration as from that of resistance). The numerical language of control is made of codes that mark access to information, or reject it. We no longer find ourselves dealing with the mass/individual pair. Individuals have become "dividuals," and masses, samples, data, markets, or "banks". Perhaps it is money that expresses the distinction between the two societies best, since discipline always referred back to minted money that locks gold as numerical standard, while control relates to floating rates of exchange, modulated according to a rate established by a set of standard currencies. The old monetary mole is the animal of the space of enclosure, but the serpent is that of the societies of control. We have passed from one animal to the other, from the mole to the serpent, in the system under which we live, but also in our manner of living and in our relations with others. The disciplinary man was a discontinuous producer of energy, but the man of control is undulatory, in orbit, in a continuous network. Everywhere surfing has already replaced the older sports." (Deleuze, 1992, p. 3)

The societies of control are characterized primarily by the control of movements, the legibility of bodies and data streams, and the modulation of individuals. Thus, individuals are not fixed and enclosed in single closed institutions but are kept in constant movement and flexibility. The techniques of domination during the Corona crisis are based on these criteria

The alleged goal is to fight the pandemic, but since this takes place in a social power space, the Corona fight with its lockdowns is oriented primarily to the cultural and recreational spheres, where everything is shut down, while the work sphere is hardly touched. The only notable known exception in Germany was the lockdown in the Gütersloh district in June 2020. In the Tönnies meat factory there, over 1553 employees had tested positive for Corona. As a result, a lockdown lasting several weeks was imposed for the district of Gütersloh (23.6.-6.7.2020). On June 24, some German states also issued accommodation bans for citizens from the districts of Gütersloh and Warendorf.

Robert Tönnies, a 50 percent co-partner in the family group, called on his uncle Clemens to resign. He said that the fact that the Group CEO had repeatedly blocked the abolition of work contracts demanded by his nephew since 2017 was one of the reasons for the outburst. In the political scandalization of working conditions in the German meat industry, which was only completed with Corona, the focus of public interest was not—otherwise this would have happened earlier—the threat to life and limb of Eastern European contract workers, but rather the protection of locals from the spread of the virus.

While the cultural and leisure sectors in Germany have been subject to a total lockdown since November 2020, the productive sector is hardly affected. While entrepreneurs are encouraged to expand home office, they are not subject to any political restrictions. Home office use was also significantly lower in the second wave than during the first wave. The enforcement patterns of traditional patterns of surveillance and domination likely play a significant role in such a trade-off among establishments. The entire manufacturing sector has not been shut down, and political demands have so far been limited to asking companies to conduct Corona tests. While students in schools are forced to take testing procedures, the principle of voluntariness prevails in the productive sector. It will not be until the end of 2021 that surveys will be conducted to determine which occupational groups are particularly affected by the pandemic. The investigations carried out to date relate primarily to family and social contacts, through which the virus is undoubtedly also passed on.

The epistemological pair of plague/cholera is contrasted in Foucault with the relationship of inclusion/exclusion, which can be used to show different social ways of dealing with and/or behaving in a differentiated way. This epistemological game can also be found in various lockdowns during the Corona epidemic. For example, tourists in Ischl (Austria) or Berchtesgaden (Bavaria) had to leave the area as potential Corona infected persons, only locals could benefit from medical treatment, the foreigners had to return to their home towns as potential carriers of transmission, which can be considered rather detrimental for a containment of the pandemic. Separations and divisions are made here, which progressively contribute to the epidemiological spread of the virus.

Border closures, for example, imply that the stranger/the other is perceived as carrying a threat. The border closures manifest this act to establish separations. In this respect, specific pairs of oppositions and groupings are established through the setting of boundaries (boundary closures). Healthy/sick, inside/outside, the native/the foreign. In this respect, the close, native transcends to the foreign/unknown, since the other could potentially be a virus carrier and the suspicion aligns the behavior. This tendency of demarcation is reinforced by the obligation to wear masks, since in it the danger, as well as the demarcation, is symbolically reflected. San Francisco and St. Louis were the major American cities that enforced mandatory mask use during the Spanish flu. These cities experienced significantly fewer deaths than other major American cities. The hazards posed by the pandemic undoubtedly require reorientation and impose significant constraints. At the same time, however, it reinforces the forms of a society of control that have been based on a dismantling of welfare-state security systems over the past 30 years, and which in themselves drive the intensification of social insecurity. The Corona virus, or rather the way society deals with the pandemic, not only reinforces such tendencies, but at the same time provides potential legitimation for the dismantling of social and individual rights.

On the one hand, the Corona virus potentially infects all people, on the other hand, it is racist and classist, since more poor people and people of color are affected by it and thus the disease pattern and mortality rate is dramatically higher among them than among the richer part of society. This is not only due to the different health insurance systems, but also to the respective housing, working and living conditions.

Even in Germany itself, double standards are systematically applied; the hygiene conditions in refugee accommodations, for example, are not remotely of the same administrative interest as those in university lecture halls, which remain closed even in the winter semester as a precaution. For it simply corresponds to the democratic logic of national state societies to place the life and survival interests of their own citizens—in this case those of every German—in case of doubt above the vital interests of migrant workers, refugees or whichever of the host countries affected by the German (by now, after all, only tourist) will to conquer. This hierarchization of "relevance to life" along state affiliations is part of the prevailing democratic consensus on which state intervention always invokes and can, indeed must, invoke.

The crisis affects everyone, but not everyone equally. While poorer households in particular bear the brunt and often suffer considerable financial losses, many super-rich are able to increase their wealth despite or precisely because of Corona. This makes the pandemic a burning glass for economic inequality.

While Corona is not the cause of existing inequalities, the current pandemic is nevertheless an amplifier of social dislocation. While many fear for their jobs or have to make ends meet with much less money due to short-time work, others continue to live in great wealth. Inequality is not only expressed in different income and wealth situations, but also in different access to health care and education or in housing conditions, which in turn decisively increases the factor of contagion.

For example, Cologne Lövenich had an incidence of 10.9 on May 12, while Cologne Gremberghoven had a 7-day incidence of 586.7 on the same day.[1]

References

Bonin, H., Eichhorst, W., Krause-Pilatus, A., & Rinne, U. (2021). *Wirtschaftliche Auswirkungen der Corona-Pandemie auf private Haushalte.* Bundesministerium für Arbeit und Soziales.

Deleuze, G. (1992). *Postscript on the societies of control* (Vol. 59). JSTOR.

[1] https://www.arcgis.com/apps/webappviewer/index.html?id=515374f75b2f4c08bbf73e05ae1239e8

DESTATIS. (2021). *Statistisches Bundesamt, Statistik Dossier: Daten zur COVID-19-Pandemie*, Ausgabe 08/2021. https://www.destatis.de/DE/Themen/Querschnitt/Corona/Downloads/dossier-covid-19.pdf?__blob=publicationFile

Federal Ministry for Economic Affairs and Energy. (2021). *2021 Annual Economic Report. Tackling the COVID-19 crisis, supporting the economic, recovery, strengthening structures*. Federal Ministry for Economic Affairs and Energy. https://www.bmwk.de/Redaktion/EN/Publikationen/Wirtschaft/2021-annual-economic-report.pdf?__blob=publicationFile&v=1

Federal Statistical Office (Ed.). (2021). *Labour costs, non-wage costs*. https://www.destatis.de/EN/Home/_node.html

Freud, S. (1919). *Das Unheimliche [The Uncanny]*. Standard Edition of the Complete Psychological Works 24 vols, In J. Strachey (Ed.) (Vol. 17). The Hogarth Press.

Goudsblom, J. (1979). Zivilisation, Ansteckungsangst und Hygiene. Betrachtungen über einen Aspekt der europäischen Zivilisationsgeschichte. In P. Gleichmann, J. Goudsblom, & H. Korte (Eds.), *Materialien zu Norbert Elias' Zivilisationstheorie* (pp. 215–253). Suhrkamp.

Jünger, E. (2013). *Der Arbeiter: Herrschaft und Gestalt*. Klett-Cotta.

Lazzarato, M. (2012). *The making of the indebted man. An essay on the neoliberal condition*. SEMIOTEXT(E).

Schmitt, C. (2021). *Politische Theologie.: Vier Kapitel zur Lehre von der Souveränität*. Duncker & Humblot.

Veblen, T. (1899). *The theory of the leisure class*. MacMillan.

Pandemic and Social Distance

Alexander Sieg

1 Introduction

Infodemie, a word coined by Gunter Eysenbach in 2000 to describe the disproportion of correct and misleading information on health and medical issues on the World Wide Web (cf. Haas, 2020, p. 51), will be a starting point for the following discussion.

For almost three years, the world was medically and socially dominated by a pandemic, which was accompanied by different state constellations of measures in different countries.

These were in confrontation with previous political and social practices, especially in Western Europe and North America, in terms of their proportionality, legitimacy and extent.

For example, traditionally the efforts of the European health authorities against influenza infections are to be classified as very moderate, having a recommendatory character.

Parallel to this, a "mass media hysteria" set in, consisting of a conglomerate of prognoses, misinformation and unprofessional analyses at the level of the feuilleton. The continuing, almost uninterrupted reporting produced manifold uncertainties with regard to appropriate social behaviour, the severity of the pandemic, and the probability of infection, not only among medical laypersons.

A. Sieg (✉)
Berlin, Germany
e-mail: alexander.sieg@gmx.de

R. D. Hepp (ed.), *Shifts and Reorientation Within the Social-Crisis and Catastrophe: Towards the Realization of Pandemic Epistemological Processes*, Prekarisierung und soziale Entkopplung – transdisziplinäre Studien,
https://doi.org/10.1007/978-3-658-43041-2_9

This article is predominantly intended to draw attention to the—in the German-speaking public—little discussed consequences of the "state of emergency", in particular to—potentially—mass social and psychological pathologies but also the increase in social inequality between and within social groupings within the social structure of Germany. In this context, the concept of social distancing plays a crucial role.

Social distancing, defined here as disparaging, cool and regulated behaviour, seems to be not only a proven means of containing a pandemic but also a vehicle of modern agile capitalism.

2 Permanent State of Emergency

Since the beginning of the Corona pandemic, the Italian philosopher and essayist Giorgio Agamben has drawn attention to its political and social implications and dangers in various columns—also in German-language daily newspapers—which, however, have not led to any significant discussion in Germany (Agamben, 2021).

Agamben refers in particular to the legal and ethical problems implied by the non-legitimised permanent state of exception with all its facets. For him, a social transformation is underway that is not based on a new legal order, but is founded on a persistent state of exception.

His thesis is that the ruling forces, i.e. the capitalistfonform forces, are using the pandemic to establish a new paradigm of how people should be governed. The old current political models, which in their view are obsolete, are no longer up to today's demands.

In the process, Giorgio Agamben continues, "biosecurity" establishes itself as a governmental dispositive, and a very powerful one at that. For when their health is potentially threatened, people accept restrictions on their freedom that they would never have endured under the yoke of totalitarian regimes. In parallel, the "right to health" turns into a juridical-religious "duty to health".

On this basis, the state of emergency is increasingly accepted as the normal state of affairs and state corona measures are not seen as repression but as rational regulations—supported by scientists, the media virologists. The fact that different approaches and paradigms exist within virology—similar to those within the social sciences—is thereby suppressed.

Apart from a few insignificant "conspirators" on the right-wing fringe of society, no serious social resistance existed or exists in the German case against measures such as the imposition of a state of emergency or exit restrictions at an arbitrarily set incidence or the wearing of an FFP2 mask according to relatively opaque criteria in public spaces.

3 Social Distance (Definition)

In the sociological context, "social distance" traditionally means an economically, culturally and structurally determined socio-spatial distance between manifest social groups as can be seen, for example, in the results of correspondence analyses as graphical representations. In pandemic occupational language, however, social distance is individualised and refers to the spatial distance of bodies including the prohibition of physical contact. In a broader sense, events such as school lessons and communications in general that are held at a distance are also understood as acts of social distance.

In our sense, social distancing is defined here as a disparaging, cool and regulated behaviour that is partially internalised and accepted unreflectively after a relatively short time.

Giorgio Agamben devotes the focus of his reflections in a text for the "Neue Zürcher Zeitung" on 8 April 2020 to "social distancing", which emerged during the Covid19 pandemic. He first postulates very carefully that "social distancing" is a euphemism to avoid the word "demarcation". He describes the pandemic as a laboratory situation in which new political and social orders are also tried out. At the same time, he concludes that a community based on "social distance" would be politically and humanly intolerable. Moreover, he works out that social distancing is inevitably linked to "passivity".

Subsequently, the question arises: To what extent has "social distancing", also as a guideline for a social order, been permanently internalised within the respective formation of a specific habitus of children, adolescents and young adults since the pandemic and still is (cf. Bourdieu, 1979, 1992). On this important point, which affects a whole generation of children and adolescents and young adults, there are no empirical studies so far and certainly no reflections from the political field on how to counteract this.

Touch/physical contact

Since the joint classic research of the British child psychiatrist and psychoanalyst John Bowlby (1907–1990) and his US-American colleague Mary Ainsworth (1913–1999) on attachment behaviour and the attachment theory developed from it, there has not only been an awareness of the importance of attachment, but also its manifestations in the sense of physical touch and contact. An important result of her research, which has been confirmed again and again by more recent research, is that physical contact and physical touch are essential factors in the development of a "secure attachment"(Bowlby, 1982).

The immense importance of physical contact between children and others, as identified in the work of Bowlby and Ainsworth and their students—which can easily be transferred to adolescents and young adults—is also an element that supports the reduction of stress and has an influence on emotional regulation.

Within psychology, so-called contagion effects are described and discussed, which cause "contagion" of behaviour and emotions in social crises. A distinction is made between social contagion and emotional contagion. While social contagion, in the tradition of Le Bon, tends to be assessed as marginal in a complex perspective, emotional contagion is determined, in particular, by reporting in social and classic media in the form of distorted risk perception, frustration, excessive demands, reluctance and feelings of fear.

If one adds to these findings elements of empirically based habitus research following Pierre Bourdieu and applies them to social psychology, then a logical consequence or option is that for example, through prolonged seclusion, the emergence of pathological forms of social distance can not only last temporarily, but can also be permanently internalised.

The basal prevention inventory of recurrent depressive illnesses includes strategies such as the prevention of loneliness or social isolation, the promotion of direct social recognition in daily routines and the reduction of stress and overload. However, it is precisely these strategic possibilities for alleviating depressive illness that were almost prevented by social distancing during the pandemic. If a depressive illness (without psychotic symptoms), as described in the ICD-10-GM (Bundesinstitut für Arzneimittel und Medizinprodukte, 2023), in addition to depressed mood and a reduction in drive and activity, also causes a loss of the ability to enjoy oneself, reduces interest and concentration, social isolation and loneliness are often causal factors in addition to an individual disposition. Pronounced fatigue can occur after the slightest exertion. Self-esteem and self-confidence are almost always impaired. Even in a mild form, thoughts about one's own worthlessness occur.

Thus, it is precisely the conditions during the period of pandemic intervention by state orders and measures or by the health authorities that are extended with regard to social distance and, consequently, according to the thesis, can lead to permanent changes in behaviour and to manifestations of depression in a considerable proportion of children, adolescents and young adults.

The depressive characteristics described are, according to the thesis, known to almost every person at the low non-pathological ranks of a scale and are usually temporary. However, persistent unfavourable social and emotional conditions can escalate them to dysthemia or manifest depressive mood.

Since, according to the report of the health insurance company DAK, employees in Germany were in any case increasingly recording days of absence due to mental illness (from 2012 to 2022, days of absence increased by 48 per cent), the number of depressed persons will, according to another thesis, increase as a late consequence of the pandemic and its consequences (for example, the so-called hybrid teaching at technical colleges and universities, which in turn—as our own observation protocols clearly show, that students, for a wide variety of reasons, opt for online teaching and the majority against face-to-face teaching)—especially of adolescents and young adults—increase significantly and thus entail a huge economic burden, also in terms of economic growth, due to lengthy absences from work and expensive hospital stays.

If, as in the pandemic world of life, for example at school or university or in the home office, human–computer interaction replaces previous social contacts and thus leads to stress, isolation and loneliness, this can in no way serve as a model for future teaching models and forms of work.

4 Two Examples: Curfew and Home Office

In the course of the ongoing pandemic, increasingly drastic regulations and measures were introduced in Germany, which—it seems—undermined the very foundations of a democratic system in their proportionality. Even the conservative German daily F.A.Z. is almost appalled by the measure of curfew restriction or "curfew" (F.A.Z., 23.04.2021, p. 15).

The strongest restrictions on personal freedom during the pandemic are the curfews. In Germany, the so-called "curfew restrictions" in the Infection Protection Act, Sect. 28, paragraph 2, have so far been subject to very high hurdles. They are only permitted if all other measures taken do not lead to effective containment.

With the amendment of the law, the curfew restrictions from 22.00 to 05.00 now came into effect with an incidence value of at least 100 on three consecutive days.

One could interpret the curfew as a collective punishment for potential immature social behaviour in the sense of not respecting social distance.

Elements of the most diverse dystopias, beginning with Jeremy Bentham (Bentham, 2013) and continuing with Michel Foucault and above all Gilles Deleuze

(Deleuze, 1990), were activated on the most diverse levels during the time of the pandemic.

Thus it is the ideas of Jeremy Bentham and their implementation in the Benthamian Panopticon that guarantees total surveillance through little effort and aims to discipline the population. Is home office, homeschooling or online teaching a modern version of Bentham's panopticon, whose central element is also social distance to prevent solidarities and communities?

Social distance, virtual isolation in front of the monitor is, according to the next observation, not least a means of surveillance and discipline. Keyword home office: What does home office mean in the sense of social distance? It means the permanent confrontation with one's own closeness with one's own face, the prolonged observation of one's own expression, one's own voice, and one's own posture. On the one hand, confrontation with and, at the same time, a decoupling from the conventional world of work, cut off from direct communication with people.

Is this a social phenomenon that merely accelerates the existing tendencies towards the transformation of social solidarities into individualisation and "isolation" and often already into virtual identities?

The social and mental effects of this process develop successively, incisively and eminently from the centre to the periphery of society. The pandemic seems to act as a catalyst for various developments that create social distances, such as the promotion of "individualised" digital nomads.

One fact is that the communicative background noise at the work and learning places that are shifted to the home is completely lost. Through home office, homeschooling or online teaching at universities, not only esteem, but also social distinctions are lost; the struggle for recognition (Honneth, 1992) loses its terrain. This is happening in a world of work that is already characterised by a progressive tendency towards precarisation and in the wake of which manifold insecure lifeworlds and living conditions are emerging (cf. e.g. Hepp et al., 2016).

The quality of collegial relationships within the working world is obviously suffering (cf. e.g. Ehlert, 2022), but this seems to be even more evident within the higher education landscape. Based on memory protocols of my own online teaching in a university, it can be stated that very often there was no discussion or exchange at all in large groups. In parallel, during the pandemic and afterwards, there was a conspicuous decline in student performance in hybrid courses and also in the courses of colleagues, both in written work and in examinations.

In many events, there was no physical feedback, only the "react" or "chat" functions in MS teams were used, especially suggesting to be present. Continuously speaking into the void for the teacher became an unusual normality. The longer this form continued, the less debates took place, fewer requests to speak and no passionate discussions as in face-to-face teaching. The few reactions of the students were characterised by a certain rationality: largely cool, objective, unemotional (Cf. also Ehlert, 2022).

At the same time, this form of teaching involved a new form of disciplining: for the students, the starting position was: microphone off! In addition, the students in larger groups were free to decide whether they wanted their physical presence to be visible through the laptop camera or whether they wanted to deactivate it. After a short time, the following happened, in the sense of the described phenomenon of the contagion effect: more and more students deactivated their camera. On the other side of the communication level, the teacher talked incessantly without any significant reaction in an empty room and into the void and was simultaneously confronted with his own mirror image.

The most emphatic losers of online teaching or of the currently frequently practised hybrid teaching are—according to my observations—so-called "introverted" students, whose status evolved from introversion to isolation and whose unstable social relationships became even more unstable.

The measures taken during the pandemic situation, the ongoing state of emergency, thus reinforces the already strong neoliberal tendencies within the world of work and life through social distance, isolation, loneliness and desolidarisation and is thus a catalyst for the advancing digital and agile capitalism. The seemingly autonomous work in the home office suggests self-determination and self-organisation, but also emancipation and self-realisation. This mobility also leads to social distance and boundless mobility in relation to other people (cf. Ehlert, 2022, pp. 39–41).

The forms of communication used in the home office (homeschooling, online teaching, etc.) are indirect communications that limit or hinder direct face-to-face encounters. In the home office, between colleagues, voice calls are considered too intrusive, there is a shift to primarily impersonal email as a form of consideration. In leisure time, the norm developed between work colleagues and also between students not to spontaneously show up at anyone's house or to call without warning. Communication thus became more free of domination within this development, but also much more distanced and superficial (cf. Ehlert, 2022: e.g. 15, 25, 37, 39, 41, 46–47, 63, 65).

As Boltanski and Chiapello (2003, French 1999) have already shown in their wide-ranging study "The New Spirit of Capitalism", flexibility, autonomy and project work are historically hard-fought achievements in the world of work, but they are radically transformed in a negative sense in the triumph of neoliberalism.

Flexibility is transformed into permanent availability, autonomy into "exploitation" of innovative ideas and project work decays as a means of pressure for follow-up jobs.

Thus, even within digital capitalism, digital work outside the office or online teaching does not lead to more autonomy and flexibility, but turns into a perfidious instrument of surveillance on the one hand, and total availability on the other.

5 Social Impact

Strongly affected by this form of social distance are single households, which have been subjected to self-isolation, exit and contact restrictions, quarantine and curfew. Following the individualisation thesis of Ulrich Beck (1986) and the social changes of the neoliberal invasion regarding precarious working and living conditions (Bourdieu, 1998), there have been successive processes of desolidarisation and drastic social distances since the 1990s anyway. In the course of the long-lasting Covid 19 pandemic, according to the thesis, an "exhausted self" emerged, especially among large parts of the younger generation, with regard to a persistent isolated individualistic self-responsibility (Ehrenberg, 2011).

In order to explore the first indications in this regard, a survey of social work students at two universities in Berlin was conducted by means of an online survey (Sieg, 2023).

The starting point was the wearing of a face mask (FFP2 mask), a textile with powerful symbolic power in the history of European and other cultures. Without discussing the symbolic power of the mask in detail here, we would like to state that the mask is considered one of the most powerful symbols of humanity. Full of aggression and fear, the mask causes identities to disappear and within this ritual leads to a personality change, albeit temporary.

In this study, the following question was asked at the beginning: How long did it take you to get used to wearing a mask, i.e. to consider it completely normal?

At first glance, the answers were very different: 9.3 per cent of the respondents said they got used to wearing a mask within 5 days, almost 13 per cent within 10 days. Up to one month was needed by 24 per cent of the respondents, up to 3 months by 27.8 percent. Longer than 3 months was needed by a small group of 7.4 per cent. An unusually large group of 16.7 per cent said they still could not get used to wearing a mask and that wearing it caused discomfort.

One possible interpretation of these first data on this problem would be that around 46 percent got used to wearing the mask very quickly—up to one month, i.e. social distance. About 52 percent needed more than one month to get used to wearing a mask and that is a very high value indeed: 24 percent of them needed a very long time or could not get used to wearing it, thus suffered from wearing a mask associated with social distance.

The masks have remained: even if it is estimated that only one in a hundred people in the Berlin cityscape currently (June 2023) wears a mask, this not only evokes memories, but also represents and actualises specific associations.

The results of the small, non-representative survey of Bachelor's students of the dual course of study Social Pedagogy and Management/Social Work support the thesis that a considerable proportion of young people are permanently marked by elements of social distance in their social behaviour.

Young people are permanently marked by elements of social distance in their social behaviour. One characteristic of social work students is their openness to working with "others", social outlaws or people who are in permanent social or psychological distress and therefore need support. Alongside the professional management of mostly individualised social problem situations is a deeply interactionist attitude and, in its wake, usually a practice that involves the opposite of social distance.

The student survey was conducted online between 23 and 25 May 2023. The population was 209 students, and the response of respondents was only registered within a period of three days. Subsequent responses were not taken into account. A total of 54 students, almost all of whom were between 20 and 25 years old, took part in the short survey. That is still 25.8 per cent of the population. The respondents were asked to answer spontaneously and briefly.

One of the questions was: Now that the restrictions have been lifted, do you behave differently or somewhat more distantly towards other people in terms of "social distance" than you did before the pandemic?

Of the students surveyed, 57.4 per cent said they behaved differently with regard to "social distance" than before the pandemic. This is a very high value despite the low representativeness of the survey.

In response to the following question (if the first answer was "yes") which behaviours in particular had been changed, these students predominantly answered that they kept more physical social distance from acquaintances and friends and especially from strangers. In addition, some students stated that they intensified their communication via social media and reduced direct personal contacts. They kept their distance on public transport or in supermarkets, and also avoided group activities and meetings in bars, cafés or restaurants, or did so less often than before the pandemic.

Typical of the respondents' answers was something like the following (interviewee 19): "greater distance from people (at cash registers, on public transport) and discomfort with too close contact with other people" and "uni rather online than in presence, as one has not come to know it "normally"".

This answer can also be considered ideal–typical: "I go out less. I tend to meet friends at home and order my food home instead of going out to eat." (Respondent 23). A final excerpt from the answers should illustrate this once again: "I notice on trains and buses etc. when it is very crowded, didn't bother me at all before, now I pay a lot of attention to distance, disinfect my hands, touch as little as possible etc." (interviewee 50).

However, none of these answers expressed genuine pathological behaviour. However, there is the potential to develop pathological patterns in dealing with "others", especially if the new, already internalised behaviours become entrenched.

Considering that these students decided before the pandemic to work in a social profession in which personal encounters between people in groups, in individual conversations and in public spaces are central, some of the students can be assessed as either not being able to work optimally in this profession or bringing too much "social distance" into their daily routine, which could or will be counterproductive in terms of the goals of social work.

On 27.01.2020, the Corona pandemic officially began in Germany. Three and a half years after the beginning of the pandemic, the undoubtedly not sufficiently representative data of a study of students shows that a slight majority has changed their behaviour with regard to social distance. The acquired greater social distance is, according to the thesis, anchored in the habitus of the students and will not change so quickly.

6 Psychopathological Effects: Stress/Anxiety/Paranoia/Depression

The "Deutsche Ethikrat" (AD-HOC recommendation of 28.11.2022) refers to the potential consequential damage of a mental nature caused by the pandemic and calls for a rapid expansion of therapy and support services, especially for children, adolescents and young adults (students). This means, as it were, that up to now there have been no or only very selective offers for the care and treatment of pandemic-related mental illnesses or impairments. Explicitly, the Ethics Council calls for a "rapid recruitment of professionals", which means that there are no professionals available for this task.

Unquestioningly, stress, anxiety, depression or even paranoia (present in Germany especially through adherents of so-called conspiracy theories, which also achieved media attention in the form of larger demonstrations) arose in many people during or in the aftermath of the Covid 19 crisis. However, it is completely unclear in which dimensions these elements of mental instability occur within the population.

This can be vividly demonstrated using the example of so-called hybrid teaching, i.e. a combination of face-to-face and online events. While students, according to my analyses based on lists of participants at one university, almost 90 percent regularly attended face-to-face events before the Covid 19 pandemic, student activity shifted to online events, which are currently preferred by about three-quarters of students.

Overall, there is a lack of comprehensive or at least random research in Germany (and also in other Western European countries and in the USA) on these potential after-effects of the pandemic. The dangers are—as already mentioned—obvious: long absences from work, high treatment costs, individual social disintegration in the form of loneliness and, as a result, high economic follow-up costs.

7 Conclusion, Discussion and Recommendations for Action

The descriptions and analyses of Giorgio Agamben (2021) show as a starting point for the considerations on lasting consequences of the Covid 19 pandemic with regard to "social distance" that seemingly irreversible changes occurred within society due to the partially contradictory actions of politics, medicine and the media during the years of the pandemic. In addition to changes in behaviour, many people experienced multiple uncertainties, insecurities and uncertainties.

It was postulated that potentially the years-long state of exception increases considerably for a whole generation of children, adolescents and young adults with regard to the widening and internalisation of social distances, and that various consequences for society arise from this. This conclusion was supported by initial evidence in a survey, but should in any case be further investigated and explored in detail and on an ongoing basis.

At the end of this brief consideration, further questions arise, such as: What role do peers or social networks take on in the internalisation of distance behaviour, or what task could they take on in dissolving or changing distance behaviour in pragmatic terms? Which social groups and social milieus are particularly susceptible or at risk with regard to the permanent adoption of elements of social distance and how can this be counteracted?

Moreover, there is no explicit empirical data on the question: To what extent has the Covid 19 pandemic permanently installed changes in everyday and working life, also with regard to "disciplining" and "surveillance and control", which in turn could also entail a reinforcement of social distances?

In his publication "Die polarisierende Pandemie" ("The Polarising Pandemic"), Christoph Butterwege (Butterwege, 2022) focuses on a double aggravation of distance: social inequality and social distance. He vividly describes the increase in social inequality in terms of health inequality and also explicitly the winners and losers of the crisis. Following this work, it would be very important to initiate further qualitative and quantitative research on the problem of social inequality.

The result in terms of changes at the level of social distance can be summarised very simply in three steps: Virtual communication in excess replaces normal communication including such elements as symbolic touching such as "shaking hands" or hugging and this successively leads to a sublime social distance.

The following central suggestions for continuing desiderata for research and initial recommendations for action now emerge from the preceding descriptions and considerations:

a) pupils, students, young adults:
b) regular larger empirical studies and samples
c) preventive therapeutic counselling and care;
d) Targeted prevention and education in social media, press, TV, public campaigns about the development and dangers of pathological or antisocial behaviour. This should be done carefully with psychological and educational means, especially education about signs of pathologies such as depression, anxiety, stress and "paranoia" and their effective professional treatment;
e) Abolition of so-called hybrid teaching in universities and return to face-to-face teaching.

References

Agamben, G. (2021). *An welchem Punkt stehen wir? Die Epidemie als Politik*. Turia+Kant.
Beck, U. (1986). *Risikogesellschaft. Auf dem Weg in eine andere Moderne*. Suhrkamp.
Bentham, J. (2013). *Das Panoptikum*. Matthes & Seitz.
Boltanski, L., & Chiapello, È. (2003). *Der neue Geist des Kapitalismus*. UVK.
Bourdieu, P. (1982). *Die feinen Unterschiede: Kritik der gesellschaftlichen Urteilskraft*. Suhrkamp.
Bourdieu, P. (1999, frz. 1992). *Die Regeln der Kunst: Genesis und Struktur des literarischen Feldes*. Suhrkamp.
Bourdieu, P. (1998). Prekarität ist überall. In P. Bourdieu (Hrsg.), *Gegenfeuer. Wortmeldungen im Dienste des Widerstands gegen die neoliberale Invasion* (pp. 96–102).UVK.
Bowlby, J. (1982). *Attachment and loss*. Basic Books.
Bundesinstitut für Arzneimittel und Medizinprodukte. (2023). Internationale statistische K.lassifikation der Krankheiten und verwandter Gesundheitsprobleme. 10. Revision. German Modification. Version 2023. https://www.dimdi.de/static/de/klassifikationen/icd/icd-10-gm/kode-suche/htmlgm2023/. Accessed June 17, 2023.
Butterwege, C. (2022). *Die polarisierende Pandemie. Deutschland nach Corona*. Beltz.
DAK. (2023). *Psychreport 2023. Entwicklungen der psychischen Erkrankungen im Job*. https://caas.content.dak.de/caas/v1/media/32628/data/3983614e98a936fe7d7dd70f3dac2e73/dak-psychreport-ergebnis-praesentation.pdf. Accessed June 17, 2023.
Deleuze, G. (1990). Postskriptum über die Kontrollgesellschaften. In G. Deleuze (Hrsg.), *Unterhandlungen 1972–1990* (pp. 254–262). Suhrkamp.
Deutscher Ethikrat (November 29, 2022). *Pandemie und psychische Gesundheit Aufmerksamkeit, Beistand und Unterstützung für Kinder, Jugendliche und junge Erwachsene in und nach gesellschaftlichen Krisen AD-HOC-EMPFEHLUNG.pdf*
Ehlert, M. (2022). *Homeoffice. Ein pandemisches Experiment*. Carl-Auer.
Ehrenberg, A. (2011). *Das Unbehagen in der Gesellschaft*. Suhrkamp.
Frankfurter Allgemeine Zeitung. (April 23, 2021). *Donnerstag*, p. 15.
Haas, J. G. (2020). *COVID-19 und Psychologie. Mensch und Gesellschaft in Zeiten der Pandemie*. Springer.
Hepp, R., et al. (Eds.). (2016). *Verunsicherte Gesellschaft: Prekarisierung auf dem Weg in das Zentrum*. Springer VS.
Honneth, A. (1992). *Kampf um Anerkennung*. Suhrkamp.
Mooney, C. G. (2010). *Theories of attachment: An Introduction to Bowlby, Ainsworth, Gerber, Brazelton, Kennell, and Klaus*. Redleaf Press.
Sieg, A. (2023). *Online-Befragung von Studierenden des Studienganges Soziale Arbeit/ Sozialpädagogik (Management) zur Auswirkung der Covid-Pandemie auf soziale Distanz(en), 22.05.2023–15.05.2023.*

Good Life and Precarization

Lennart Noerreklit

1 Introduction

The power to survive and win in the short run by destroying the conditions for the good life, in the long run, is the power to self-precarize and lead to self-destruction. We have created societies that produce massive destruction of life, including human life and living conditions. Our short-term endeavors to make a good life produce long-term deteriorating living-conditions. In our development of society, we have destroyed whatever life we believed in our way. Thereby we caused worsening living conditions. It appears that we are about to precarize our situation. Humans have the power to self-destroy. Presumably, we do not want to do that. But do we have the power that is needed to avoid doing it?

The last generation has proclaimed itself. Although the proclamation is exaggerated, we have created precarious conditions. Although the deterioration has been visible for many decades, human societies have not been motivated to stop the destructive behavior and do anything practical to prevent this from happening.

Can we activate previously inactivated resources to make a turnaround that overcomes this process of self-precarization?

This discussion reflects the troubling sides of modern society. It reflects its dark story, not the whole story. At the edges of the good life, there is decay and death. Death attracts death. As an eco-philosopher may claim that life loves life, she may also think death loves fear and death. Why else would humans produce

L. Noerreklit (✉)
University of Aalborg, Aalborg, Denmark
e-mail: falselennartnorreklit@gmail.com

R. D. Hepp (ed.), *Shifts and Reorientation Within the Social-Crisis and Catastrophe: Towards the Realization of Pandemic Epistemological Processes*, Prekarisierung und soziale Entkopplung – transdisziplinäre Studien,
https://doi.org/10.1007/978-3-658-43041-2_10

so much of it? One cannot avoid dying, but one could at least avoid maximizing it through continuous warfare and destroying the ecosphere.

Maybe the experience of suffering and death within a living person causes a desire for death and destruction. Ordinary people do not desire this destruction. It comes from the leaders—politics, industry, media, and the military. History has many stories of industrial and military powers manipulating political opinions to green light destruction and death. Why did the leaders want to do that? Could they find nothing better to do? There are so many other positive values of life and prosperity that they could contribute to. There must be something dark in them that makes them do these things instead of doing something life-friendly. And all their henchmen, could they not find anything better to do? Is this their values, their ethics, their smartness, their character? Since they replace life-friendly behavior with destruction and death, one cannot but conclude that they lack a life-friendly ethos. Instead, the ethos they induce in society is life-hostile and involves control, oppression, destruction, and death. The population is living beings and can but be precarized by a life-hostile ethos. The leaders themselves are living beings and can but be precarized by the ethos they induce. The destruction they produce causes widespread social precarization amongst all their victims. But they are kept prisoners of their dark notions wherever they come from. Maybe the notions are religious or popular 'science' like the social Darwinist imagination that progress is due to outcompeting and destroying the others. They forgot what the dark lesson from National Socialism is. They also ignored the scholarly criticism of naturalistic ethics, such as in social Darwinism (that out-competing the other is good), that it is biased on unscientific is also suddenly forgotten.

What else are the motives driving this evil? Is it an evil nature of humankind? Then there is little hope. Or is it a historical condition that a confrontation with the emerging consequences can change? That would give room for hope. Then, people and leaders can become wiser and choose a life-friendly-ethos.

A person may feel insecure about losing her job or a partner and be concerned about what to do. This experience is typical. A healthy person feels the pain but can overcome it. She eventually creates new relations, engages in new interactivities, and re-integrates into community structures. She does this because she is socially healthy. She emanates no 'smell' of rotten flesh that stigmatizes her—externalizes her inner precarity and chases others away so she is lost in precarity and social pain. She becomes awkward and socially displeasing to the 'in' people. Her wounds make her movements weird and seemingly irrational. She may try to hide and internalize her weirdness. She may discover that it scares people, which makes her tuff. She may become aggressive and inflict pain on others.

In a good society, socially healthy people protect and help a wounded person. They love life, like to help, and do not like to see her suffer. They recognize the wounded child whose trauma already precarizes it, as they also recognize the precarious adult that lost her bonds of love, etc.

There are precarious people everywhere in a precarious—i.e., sick-society. They have all kinds of diagnoses and feel constantly tense about life. They do not experience life-friendliness. They are anxious that they will not make it. Or they have given up. In this society, a 'healthy' person is also in trouble—assuming she still exists. Her empathy calls her to help all the suffering she sees. But that is impossible. She must choose to help some and abstract from all the others. To do that, she must blind empathy to their suffering. She must wear a 'gas mask' to avoid the smell and protect her good life, health, and ability to help. Some create living quarters where there is no bad smell. Some become part of the disease. Some eventually hate the wounded for their smell. They begin to claim that the precarious people themselves are at fault. If they still have ethics, such claims make them feel guilty and bad about themselves. And this feeling may make them hate even more. They signal their disgust through avoidance. Their ethics erode. There is no help to precarious people. The 'healthy' people lost their life-friendly ethics, became precarious, and could not be good people although they lived in better conditions.

A socially healthy person has compassion and feels the commandment to ease the suffering of her neighbor, like the good Samaritan. If just one Lazarus suffered, then she could be the helping Samaritan. But society is filled with wounds and suffering, as is seen in joyless busying and in the tensed voices. Everybody wears a gas mask and darkened glasses to avoid experiencing the ocean of precarization. Therefore, they only see a busy society with good positive people.

Jesus' parable of the good Samaritan depicts a world with only a few precarious people. The Samaritan only met Lazarus. Were there fewer precarious people then than now? Probably not. But the parable has no advice on deciding whom the Samaritan should help if he meets many Lazarus's. The Samaritan found Lazarus outside the city, outside the community. Thus his community could not help him. Lazarus is precarized like those expelled from the community. The problem is that people within the society are expelled and precarious. There are many lonely people and social Lazarus's. How can one solve this problem?

For some time, the idea of the social knowledge society could serve as a solution. Everybody should follow the Platonic ethos of skill and knowledge. When people act based on knowledge, then they can produce solutions to the world they love. People contribute and give. Precarious people are getting help. It only needs good leadership to coordinate the many skilled people. Socially healthy people have a giving nature. A healthy person is not controlled by greed and craving. That is addiction, and addicted people are precarized. The ability to produce and give is healthy and based on knowledge and a life-friendly ethos. It is easy for leaders to coordinate work in an environment with a life-friendly ethos because people like to do good things.

The ethos of this life-friendly knowledge society organizes good living conditions that protect people against precarization. People develop skills to contribute and trust that society also will help them. They live in the good knowledge society, the best society ever. It is not as perfect as Leibniz's vision of the logically best of all worlds, but it seems to be the best society in history.

Paradoxically, today where we possess so much knowledge, this vision does not apply to our society. Despite all the knowledge, so-called democracy, human rights, and 'the great peace,' there are many terrible social acts. People are stressed and have problems. Our societies produce destruction, death, and precarization on a massive scale. The knowledge society, democracy, peace, and human rights are fiction. Millions of refugees, often fleeing due to the baseless destruction of their countries by our attack or support for violent conflicts. Even the whole biosphere is becoming precarious due to our behavior. Our Western societies do these things. They do it deliberately, not by accident. They must have known what they did. They had engineers and professionals that were well-educated. In addition, research has documented destructive effects for a long time. Sometimes it has been documented that industries financed deception to halt regulation to stop detrimental activities. Ordinary people did not want these things to happen. Leaders made it happen. They presumably wanted to do good but created destruction and precarization. They are ordinary people and, thus, probably neither sillier nor more malicious than most others. Thus they must be precarized. They seem to be led by notions that blind them. They do not know what life-friendliness is and should vouch for that.

The message of this chapter is that the good life, the goal of all activities, presupposes a life-friendly ethos. Social precarization is the result of a life-hostile ethos. Most important to a society is the ethos of its leaders. A society controlled by precarized leaders cannot act based on a life-friendliness ethos. It is in a terrible situation. It is doing horrible things. Its people are precarized by the illusions this society produces.

The first part of the chapter discusses what it means that precarization is the precarization of life. Precarization destroyed the good life. Life is characterized by a special form of activity, namely self-activity. This self-activity solves life's problems by establishing communities of cooperating, self-active people. Being a self involves the other. Everybody contributes and gives something special. This is what the self likes. It is social. Through these activities and relations, people have identity and intrinsic, non-replaceable value to each other. Precarization is losing these attributes. The second part addresses some of the social techniques, motives, and consequences involved in precarization. The focus is on communicative tools to strengthen common self-activity or destroy self-activity and cause precarization.

2 Value Perspectives

A value perspective is necessary for the analysis to be relevant to social activities. If the perspective is that of special funding interests, then research becomes biased. Being biased it aims at precarizing the other who therefore is a victim of the bias. Nothing can argue against science. On the other hand, if there is no perspective as some research leaders demand, then it has no relevance. This dilemma applies to research in precarization. Either a value perspective is outlined, and research serves particular interests at the expense of the victims. Or the analysis is 'neutral' and 'value blind,' a description of neutral facts only containing no reference to values and justification for any activity. Against a 'neutral, objective approach,' it is argued that it presumably is an illusion. Arguments are used to demonstrate that values are subjective, thus essentially biased and outside the range of rational scientific analysis. Such a position is backed by positivist arguments ('proofs') such as Hume's guillotine and G.E. Moore's open question argument. Without a proper value perspective, scientific valuation, and re-evaluation of social values, science can describe and analyze facts only. G. Myrdal thus suggested the solution that researchers must define their subjective value perspective when defining their research projects.

However, Myrdal's solution is not satisfactory. It appears to accept bias in research when it is visible because it is inevitable. However, science is problematic if it serves interests other than the truth about the values it analyzes. It is a mistake to identify subjectivity and bias. The scientific methodology should prevent bias, not by doing irrelevant research but by using a comprehensive, versatile perspective on values. This perspective is inclusive and considers the value perspectives of all those whose values are affected. Research replaces a chosen and, therefore, a biased perspective of those in power with a comprehensive—thus unbiased—perspective of all affected, inclusive of the precarious. Affected parties must be heard so that their views are represented fairly. The ambition of a comprehensive approach is a condition for unbiased relevance for all projects and reporting. Such change would seriously limit the possibilities of legitimizing destructive behavior and pave the basis for a significant reduction of precarity on a global scale.

The fundamental arguments against the possibility of an unbiased perspective on values, such as the open question argument, have a point. They do demonstrate that moral concepts such as 'goodness' or 'the good' have no observable reference, and do not therefore point out a possible object of a scientific description. Values are outside the world of facts and events, the factual world, the young Wittgenstein states. That is why they cannot be empirically defined as proven by the open-question argument. That is why science cannot study them.

This inference is however mistaken, because it is a mistake that such a reference is needed. Practice is neither concerned with "the good" nor "goodness." Nobody can find such entities in the world. That is correct. Looking for the good is a naming fallacy in the sense of the late Wittgenstein. "Good" is not a word used to refer to a specific object. Its meaning is not its reference—it has none. Its meaning is its use, and it is not used to refer to any object. It has several usages, but it is basically used to express comparisons and thereby evaluate objects and phenomena compared to similar objects. These objects must be observable and comparable, and the comparisons must be based on observations.

Concerning precarity: There is nothing subjective in considering precarization as a problem. Precarity is by definition a problem, i.e., something bad/not good to the living creature in a precarious situation. A precarious situation of a person is a situation, where the person is unable to cope with her situation compared to a non-precarious situation where she can cope. Contrary to Moore's claim that there is no analytic relation between the concept of goodness and real phenomena, the concept of precarity manifests such a relation! The concept of precarity by itself overcomes Moore's open-question argument. It did so without referring to any special phenomenon of goodness. It did so by attaching the concept of good/bad to the concept of life thus comparing different conditions of human life.

For something to be good or bad, it must be something specific in the world, and it must be good or bad for some living creature. In the case of precarization, it is, by definition, not good for a precarized entity. In this, there is no bias.

3 Life–Value, and Precarization

There is, however, a phenomenon that should be good, namely life. Thus the value perspective is the good life. "Life," including "good life" and "poor or bad life," are expressions referring to real phenomena. It is, therefore possible to compare good and poor or bad life in many scholarly ways. Thus there is a value perspective in research on precarization as in most other social studies.

All life and only life can be in a precarious situation. How precarization specifically works out depends on the type of life. Lifeless physical systems can only metaphorically be in a precarious situation. The 'precarious' situation of a star that is about to collapse and become a supernova does not mean anything to the star. Nobody cares unless some astronomers are studying it.

The meaning of "good" in "good life" is determined by the kind of life. While it is absurd to look for goodness in itself, observing and studying the good life of specific living creatures is meaningful.

Further, most people possess a lot of knowledge about what constitutes and produces a good life. They could not survive without it. All activities are guided by ideas on how to produce good living conditions. If the ideas are mistaken, the person is in a precarious situation.

The time horizon of precarization is significant. Whether something is just a challenging event or a precarizing trauma depends on its effect on the involuntary and painful changes in the storyline of life. That a person, for a short period, for instance, has no job is insignificant if it is easy to find a new job. Although it may appear to the victim that she is in a precarious situation, in reality, she is not because she can solve the problem by self-activity. But if this is not the case—either because there are no jobs or because being once excluded makes it impossible to return. It is even important to how she is affected by her unemployment situation, without a partner or otherwise excluded. If it does not affect her, she may be able to reintegrate because she shows no subtle signs of being excluded and thus not showing signs of being unsocial. She may still intuitively be recognized as part of the social community. If, however, she is vulnerable, affected by the situation, and doubts whether she can re-integrate, then her subjectivity makes her precarious. Her insecurity and negative feelings may make it difficult to reintegrate. Her social wound is noticeable in her behavior.

Based on experience and self-activities, a person produces a story of life as her life. Traumas disrupt her storyline. Traumata are situations where she is helpless and in danger. Trauma are produced in precarious situations. This internalized precarity follows the person as a social wound. Trauma and precarization go hand in hand. Traumata disrupt the storyline of life. They stay in the person like a hidden disease that can always break out again and create new disruptive precarizing events.

4 Activity

Life is characterized by activity. If its activities do not function, then it is precarious. Specifically, the activity of a living being is a dynamic self-activity. A living being maintains life by producing the necessary conditions for life through its activities. When its activities stop, it dies. This applies to human beings as to any other living being.

The activity of living beings differs from the movements of non-living phenomena such as wind or waves. Unlike non-living nature, living beings act and interact selectively—deliberately—to maintain and continue life.

If the activities of a living being function well in the sense that they produce the conditions needed for living, then the being has power and is in control of its life. Power and precarity are opposites. Accordingly, there are the following precarious situations in which the living being lost its power to produce the conditions of life.

1. precarization by incapacitation (disease, accident): It cannot act. The being is on the brink of death.
2. precarization by exclusion: It can act, but its activities do not have the power to produce conditions for living. The being is in a precarious situation and will soon die unless it gets help.
3. precarization by alienation: It can act effectively, but other living beings control its living conditions and dictate what it must do to obtain them. It lacks the freedom to control its activities. It is the subjugated part of a master–slave relationship p. Its activities serve the purpose of a master. This is a precarious situation. Its life depends on the 'good will' of a master who decides what it must do. It is alienated from its activities. It is not in power.

When the power is lost, the living being will soon die unless it gets help.

4.1 Integration Versus Precarity

People that are incapacitated cannot actively produce values. Similarly, precarization by exclusion does not contribute to producing values. This is a loss. They can produce values but are prevented from doing so by being excluded. It must be an advantage to society to reintegrate them. However, people precarized by alienation are actively producing value for society. They are precarized because they do not control what they are doing. The role of the excluded people is to keep the alienated motivated because they also fear becoming expelled.

For a person to be in power to successfully self-control her activities so that they fulfill the purpose of creating a good life, she needs to integrate the constitutive conditions for her acts to have power so that her activities function. Following pragmatic constructivist analysis, these are:

1. She must possess adequate knowledge of the factual conditions of the world that she can access. If she only acts based on guesses, she will likely fail at some point.
2. She must know about possibilities she can realize through her activities. Thus she must know what possibilities different things (phenomena, institutions, people) possess and can be made accessible through her action. By combining her factual knowledge with her knowledge of the potential possibilities of phenomena, she constructs ideas of her factual possibilities. These are the things she can do.
3. She must be aware of the values she pursues and that they are constitutive of the food life for her. She then needs to integrate her values and her factual possibilities. If she recognizes that her values are outside her factual possibilities then she has a problem. She must either enlarge her possibilities through learning. Or she must influence her values by opening for developing new values. If she can neither, then she is in a precarious situation. However, the world contains many loveable things, people, other living beings, arts, and events. Therefore, it should be possible to develop values. The problem is that values are controlled by society, and she needs to augment them or affect them with her activities. If she is expelled, she is excluded from these activities.
4. She must be able to communicate her integrated perspective with other people. Society controls all, and access operates through communication. Communication is the difference between the social and the not social.

Strategies that influence power versus precarization concern these four conditions. A person needs access to resources and ideas for producing good conditions.

Society controls the resources. Thus she needs society to grant her access to resources. Resources generate factual conditions to realize possible values. A resource is an integrated unit. Societies may struggle to keep resources under control despite imperialist threats from other societies. This may precarize the whole population. Within the society, its members may struggle to access resources and avoid precarization by exclusion. The cost may be accepting precarization by alienation.

Social power is based on communication, the social glue between people. To be included in social networks and avoid exclusion, the ability to communicate is the tool at hand. To cope with the social power, she needs to understand how her communication works and what it does to her situation.

4.2 Complementarity and Self

Living beings interact with the environment to live. Living beings cooperate with other living beings to survive and propagate. Life can only exist by interacting with other living beings, intra- and inter-species. Human beings are inherently social in organizing their life with other people. Through cooperation, they organize resources and activities to make the community thrive. They do this by developing synergetic relations. Synergetic relations create contributions that complement each other to produce good life conditions. Cooperation is mostly doing things that complement what others do to produce a whole. Organizing a chain of complementary activities calls for creativity and adaptivity on all fronts. Developing self through complementary interaction creates a community and makes the relationship social. People are not only active, but they are also self-active. The will to act comes from within themselves as living beings. But what they want to do comes from their interaction experience where they discover themselves with different others and build notions of each active being as a special self. Small children may even project a self into things. The complementary interplay between the network of living beings, each with a self that acts and relates to the other, constitutes the social character of the relations. This interaction inspires creativity. The curiosity: 'How will the others react to my idea?' This calls for producing an inspiring action and for expecting a creative response. The creative complementary interplay is fun and creates the dynamics of social life.

If there were no complementarity, people would do the same, and there would be no social life. People could not develop a sense of self. They would all be the same kind of person.

The complementarity in interaction invigorates a sense of self and self-activity, producing bonding. Lasting relations in which the image of the other is part of oneself. Through bonding, people become irreplaceable to each other. They structure a meaningful life by relational bonding. Bonding develops complementary interaction by developing co-narratives in which people adapt different roles and personal identities of significance to the group and community. This creates a cohesive community with a web of bonds organized by the web of co-narrations.

In this world, people experience their value not as needy receivers but as generous givers. Their pride is to be able to give. People like to give. It makes them happy. Complementary relations imply that all participants are actors that produce something for others. People feel good about giving contributions to others. The community web regulates these patterns of interaction. This realizes more intelligence and care than control by singular persons can provide.

The opposite to this mature social attitude of giving people is an attitude of neediness, where people set their own needs and desires up front, not concerned about the desires of others. Neediness turns to greed because there is no end to the need. There is no end to the need because it provides no satisfaction. Satisfaction comes from giving and experiencing that the gifts are received and contributes to a good environment and a good life. Mature people create meaning and satisfaction through their generous contribution to contribute to a good life.

Bonds develop through interaction. People learn to know and understand each other. The knowledge of the other becomes a part of and influences oneself. Thus it is bonding. As their knowledge grows, they adapt to and feel inspired by each other. Their cooperation develops so that they complement each other. Everybody develops something special. This makes cooperation richer and everybody something special. By being in a giving position, they mature, create trustworthiness, and are happy. A benevolent person is happy because she feels that she does something valuable. That is what she wants to do. She receives what she needs. So she is not needy. She trusts that her environment, which she loves, supports her. Which they will if the relations are normal and healthy.

Mutual liking and bonding through complementary activities make people direct their self-activity to contribute. Bonding and liking produce such complementary self-activity. In such relation, people do what they like to do. And when it comes to things that somebody must do but none like to do, they nevertheless like to help the group and contribute to the solution.

This is the foundation of people's unique, irreplaceable value to each other. The complementarity in relational bonding makes people unique and irreplaceable values to each other in a web of liking, bonding, and understanding. The death or disappearance of an irreplaceable partner is a cause of sorrow, a wound that needs to heal.—If the loss was not severe, then there was no bonding, and people had no irreplaceable value to each other. Their relation s was superficial. They had not developed an inter-human relationship as part of a good life. Being replaceable units to each other means that cooperating produces little trust, fun, and feeling well. It would be wasting a part of their lives.

Nevertheless, in present society, people are becoming increasingly replaceable. Demand for standard behavior replaces more and more the self-activity of competent professionals. Modern information technology is used extensively and in many ways to transform self-activity into alienated activity, making it replaceable. Centralized control is not compatible with self-activity because that is difficult to replace, thus limiting the central power. Although it is effective and creates dynamics, it is not wanted. Thus people are alienated from their work. The self-ness of activities is lost. They are in a precarious situation that is less visible, and the precarity of people that are excluded from the chains of interaction. They do things that have nothing to do with their will and desire. They are easy to replace at work, in partnership, parenthood, professions, and living places. They are instruments. Somebody can replace them, and nobody will miss their contribution.

We live in a society of the replaceable. In it, relations cannot be trusted. In it people live under the stressed threat of being replaced, bonds are too shallow to bind, they are not good enough for others to want them, or they do not trust and like others enough to be with them. There is fear of losing one's bonds and being unable to create bonds that produce a good life. People are replaceable as lovers, parents, children, teachers, as employees, etc. People are social beings. They need bonding to develop self-activity and mean something. But they are replaceable. They cannot change that fact. They are in a precarious situation. Even in speech, people seem to fear losing their relationship with the other. People speak as fast as they can to not be too slow and boring and lose the attention of the other. The spirit of the precarious society constantly vibrates the message to people that 'it does not matter what you do—if you go, another takes your place—you are replaceable, you are nothing.'

To a society of replaceability, the quality of self-ness in the self-activity of the good life is a problem because it involves bonding. Bonding produces self-active networks that accumulate power. This is beneficial for democracy. But it limits the possibilities for centralized power to control society. Thus it increases its ability to control by increasing the level of replaceability.

The exclusion from the social web may be the basic form of social precarization. Excluded people tend to lose their bonds, access to factual resources, and shared values. Their very words lose their meaning because they are only words and not connected to social cooperation. Their life loses its worth because they have almost nothing to give. Social life bypasses them.

The threat of precarity by exclusion creates fear that causes many people to self-precarize by abstaining from self-activity, over adapt and thus self-alienating. Stress may be a different form of precarization. When people still believe in their personal goals, activity, and good mission and believe that they live in the good knowledge society, they may fight hard to reach the good life goals that motivate them as mature benevolent people. At the same time, the system makes it increasingly impossible to realize the goal no matter how hard they work. The stress changes their personality, and they become sick. They did not possess adequate know-how of the social forces of their society. Their empathy, love of life, and disbelief that the good society could be cynical made their situation precarious.

It is a severe problem that social power precarizes many people in society. Worst is, however, the destruction and suffering and millions of refugees caused by hate propaganda and war faring for several decades, destroying country after country. And social power produces an even greater destruction of life because it precarizes the very living conditions on Earth by killing countless other life forms and polluting air, water, and soil.

Signs of a good life are thriving, dynamic self-activity, adaptability, and complementarity. These signs are evident and observable. Therefore, they can be studied and analyzed, and research can produce knowledge about the good life.

Furthermore, since many resources are available because it is a wealthy society, it is a puzzle why people accept precarization and disempowerment. Why accept fear, worry, and sorrow over losing deep relations? Why is the warmth of the heart not preventing this? Why do people accept to produce death and destruction through constant wars due to warmongering politics? And why do they accept the industrial economy's systematic destruction of living conditions? All these losses are known and caused by human behavior. Why does anyone want to do this? Why do this in the richest, most knowledgeable, and presumably best society ever?

A democracy would change this self-induced unease of mind about who we are and promote happiness with fellow human beings in the near and far environment. The Devil is neither Fate, an angry God, aliens, nor the other life forms on Earth. It is social power. It is the governance that decides and the cowardness of people that accepts.

4.3 Active and Passive

There is a common dualistic mindset that distinguishes between those who are the subjects and active and those who are the objects and passive. The objects must be manipulated to be motivated to do things. The subjects are those in power, the leaders. The objects are those they lead. This view underlies theories of power and control, management, and leadership. This mindset outlines an asymmetric power relation, a master–slave dialectics manifested in centralistic power hierarchies. This dualistic mindset is basic to the legitimization of precarization. Passive people are natural objects of precarization.

This dualist mindset has also played a role in interpreting professionals as knowledgeable and active, who treat their clients as receptive and passive. The point is that the actors must be those with knowledge. However, since it is common knowledge that life is self-active, this asymmetry has been reduced. Now the role of the professional often is to provide the client with the knowledge to become active again.

Associated with this dualist mindset is the notion that happiness is a particular state of passive receptivity in which 'the good experience of happiness' comes to people. That explains why people want to relax and feel happy by doing nothing except sitting and enjoying. This is a mistaken view of happiness. Happiness comes from being self-active and succeeding in bringing the people and things one loves to flourish. This adds irony to the precarization: the people that are precarized and therefore passive are even absurdly claimed to be rewarded by enjoyment and happiness. This mad perception of 'unfairness' towards those in power by those precarized and passive demonstrates, to some, an unfairness against those in power who work hard to manage things. This unfairness legitimizes extraordinary rewards to compensate those in power, poverty, and bad conditions for the precarized.

That life is self-active means that there is no life-form of being passive. The fact that life is activity contradicts any notion that some humans are inherently lazy and need the motivation to become active. Such notions demonstrate life forgetfulness. Life is self-active. It does things. Denying this has behavioral consequences. If values are not about life but about passivity, then they are about death. Life-forgetfulness is an entrance to the rule and value of death-wars, destruction of the biosphere, life in stress, and precarization.

Rest and relaxation may be confused with passivity. Resting serves the purpose of recovering and is only apparently passive. Rest is an internal activity in which the body recovers from the wear and tear caused by the preceding external activities. There is no distinction between being active and being passive but between external activities where people engage with the environment and on the other hand internal activities in which the body focuses on repairing, recovering, and rebuilding itself. What socially is recognized as an activity are the external activities. They are made possible by internal activities. Rest is not passivity but important internal activity to rebuild the body so that the person recovers and stays strong, balanced, and in top form. The circadian rhythm controls the daily change between external and internal repair activities. Conditions that force a person to sideline her circadian rhythm, for instance, in long-term stress, precarizes the person. It harms her ability to self-act and control what she is doing and undermines her mental and physical health. The common life form of permanent stress induces an ongoing element of precarization.

The goal of life is not to be passive, either. Happiness is not being passive. People living a good life are not passive. The truth is the opposite. As all living beings, people enjoy self-activity, deciding and controlling what they do.

Imaginations like 'the bliss of being passive' are a dualist vision of being something more than a living creature, as being something over and above the mere living body. This narrative is, for instance, used to overcome feelings of fear and guilt of soldiers and to comfort their dear ones if they get killed in battle. However, all living beings, including people, live by being active. When activity stops, they are dead. It is while being alive they should have a good life based on their self-activity with others.

Some people may mistake meditation for a passive state. On the contrary, it is a state in which the person detaches from all the stresses of the environment, which enables her to achieve peace of mind and augments her internal rebuilding of strength and balance, overcoming the destructive burden of her worries. Meditation is not passive. It detaches from the external environment but balances and strengthens internal activities.

Healthy people may be passive because their self-activities have no power because they are not allowed the power to succeed. Thus they are prevented from accomplishing things the person desires. Other people, especially gatekeepers, reject their endeavors. Their passivity is, therefore, forced, a state of precarization. The cause of this passivity is that the social powers they encounter, do not accept this self-activity. Social control causes passivity when the victims feel they cannot succeed by being self-active because the social forces are against it. This control may give them a choice between precarization by alienation or exclusion: act like a robot, controlled by others, and therefore no longer live like a living human whose brain is born hard-wired to control her activities based on her desires, analysis, and decisions. A different choice is precarization by exclusion. There is a third choice, to be passive, make no choice, demonstrating resilient resistance by passivity.

To be in the power of one's life and avoid succumbing to precarization, one must integrate the four aspects: a factual base, available possibilities, values, and communication. This integration is a unique construct for each person. It is based on experience and the person's reflection and testing of ideas for living. If integration of these conditions is not realized, then her activities have no power.

She may be able to do something by using her body to move and speak, but the result will be arbitrary. She is precarized. She is like a paralyzed person that wants to move her arm but discovers that nothing happens although she tries to move it. Her moving around and doing things accomplish nothing. Since resources and possibilities are socially controlled, she may eventually discover that she fails because social powers will not allow her to succeed. This experience that social power will not give her a chance can make her passive. She lacks the knowledge of how to change the mind of the gatekeepers. She lacks the knowledge of needed social communication.

Communication provides the ability to interact with others and to agree on integrating facts, possibilities, and values to set and realize shared goals. Communication is especially important to the production of precarization. If one of these conditions is missing, then the outcome of activities is out of control, unpredictable, and random. The situation of people is precarious. They can only hope that luck is on their side. Therefore, research needs methods to recognize and integrate factual conditions, possibilities, values, and communication in order to produce knowledge of how to empower activities and create a good life.

Being in power is the integration of factual possibilities, values, and communication. Precarity is disintegration. Being able to integrate is being able to avoid precarization. Successful self-activity organizes integration that enables the person to obtain a good life. The signs of a good life are common to living beings. They flourish and thrive if they are healthy and have good conditions in which they unfold their self-activity and are appreciated by their environment. The signs of thriving and flourishing are common and obvious: a high degree of activity, a good joyful spirit, no excessive fear and stiffness, no hiding and aggression, but concentration and energy, laughing, and generally giving inspiration and joy to their environment. One feels it immediately, whether people thrive or are upset and in a precarious condition. Whether animals or plants thrive or are in miserable conditions is similarly noticeable.

There are many ways for dominant social power to precarize subordinates or relatives by preventing them from achieving integration.

There is no valid basis for a dualist division of people into subjects and objects. Such dualist thinking is the basis for discrimination and oppression or aggression. All people are subjects and objects. The illogical nature of such dualism leads to paranoiac social patterns. It creates perceptions of truth and good values being a priori on the side of 'the subject.' It creates fiction of inside and outside enemies to the good society to produce fear and wage wars. It uses a thousand-year-old storyline that almost defines human culture: "I/we are good, but you /they are bad. And must be destroyed." This storyline has legitimized the most horrific actions of mass murder (i.e., war) and destruction. It is, however, this storyline that is bad. Scientific analysis should replace it.

This storyline exemplifies master–slave dialectics. It overlooks that it is not only the slave that is precarized. The master is also precarized. She is caught in this dialectic, believing that her power and wealth give her a good life. She may overlook that she does not thrive and feel happy and generous. These are feelings that belong to a good life. Instead, her role as master forces her into a life of forgetfulness, making her life precarious.

The subject-object divide is logically a form of complementarity. But it is not a good one because it is not social. It does produce a bonding. But again not a good one. The master–slave relation terminates dialogue and the interactivity that characterizes mutual social bonding. No self-identity is created, only the relation of robbing the slave of her power and subjugating her to her master. The mature form of benevolent interaction by giving is replaced by taking as much and giving as little as possible.

5 Precarization and Knowledge

If a person's ideas on how to act do not integrate the constitutive conditions, they lead to failures and precarization. What she needs is knowledge. Without sufficient relevant knowledge, a person is precarized. The relevant knowledge encompasses the four conditions and how they can be integrated: knowledge of the situation, possibilities, and values, and how to communicate.

The knowledge needed is know-how. It is not sufficient to know. It must be knowledge that positions the person and concerns her situation and possibilities. It will help her to get knowledge from something other than a textbook or a Google search. She must be able to integrate it into her situation to develop her own know-how. This development and integration of knowledge is a creative cognitive work in which the person develops her personality and unique self as an actor. It is the basis of self-activity, where she uses her know-how to realize her ideas. Her knowledge is her power to avoid precarization. If her knowledge of her factual situation is vague or mistaken, then her ideas may not lift off. If her vision of possibilities is unrealistic, her activities will not realize them. If her understanding of the values is bad, then realizing them does not lead to the happiness she expected, causing her to be disappointed and demotivated. All this makes it difficult to assert herself as an acting person. Thus her life as self-active being is precarious. If she cannot rectify these things by communicating with others, her environment stops trusting her. They alienate her by sidelining her needs for information, limiting her access to possibilities, and participating in developing values. Initially, they may alienate her by using her to do secondary things. This may eventually lead to an exclusion. Lack of knowledge in the form of relevant know-how causes disintegration. Disintegration causes activities to become powerless. This leads to social alienation and exclusion.

By the act to precarize I mean the activity of disrupting the power to self-act, thereby causing the precarious situation of a victim. The precarizing actors are social gatekeepers. These are leaders and their henchmen. However, self-precarization is also a phenomenon. All the way, in a precarization process, there may be implicit negotiations where a victim guides herself out in precarious positions. The reasons for this may be many. For instance, she may not accept alienation and prefer exclusion. She may even consider exclusion as her way of punishing the system and its gatekeepers. In the extreme, suicide may sometimes have this character.

5.1 Social Knowledge

If someone knows how to integrate into social networks, she can avoid becoming a victim of precarizing acts. Thus the main precarization factor is a lack of knowledge about social integration. Most people have an intuitive know-how of how to integrate. However, conditions for integration are not static. Society changes, and with it the conditions for integration. What once was good know-how may become outdated. A society in the turmoil of chaotic changes has not one but several ways to integrate and exclude people. There is a skill to recognize the conditions and adapt or reject them. Some people understand integrative mechanisms in a way that enables them to integrate into different cultures. Other people have difficulties integrating even in their own culture. Their experiences may have caused them to reject the conditions needed to be integrated. Suppose, for instance, a person is a child in a minority that experienced discrimination. In that case, the pain of discrimination and the loyalty to her offspring may cause her to reject integrative behavior and consider it unacceptable subjugation to oppression. She may choose to be in a precarious position because she belongs to a subgroup with which she tries to integrate. Precarized groups provide a safe no-prepared home to people precarized by society.

The know-how needed to avoid being precarized as a living being is a knowledge of how to produce values by self-activity in the given circumstances. This knowledge includes know-how that enables the person to communicate effectively with other actors to produce integration and force gatekeepers to accept them and (re)integrate them.

The amount of precarization indicates that there is all abundant 'social' knowledge and research concerning how to control people, making them precarious objects of manipulation, while the opposite research, how for vulnerable people to counter manipulation and threats of precarization, appears less compelling. It is not only the knowledge of the victim that inevitably signals her subjective precarious status, but that is also insufficient. The general cultural understanding of how communication can help bypass and overcome stigmatizing communication needs improvement. The many precarious people that are visible are not taken seriously. This lack of know-how precarizes all people. They do not know what to do. The many issues of precarious people weaken their ethics by forcing them to overrule their feeling of empathy to maintain a social practice.

5.2 A Knowledge Society

The world might be full of resources and possibilities; if a person does not know this, she is in a precarious situation. This condition calls for the idea of a knowledge society. The world is rich in resources. Precarity is the absence of relevant knowledge! A knowledge society organizes the production, distribution, and usage of needed knowledge.

The idea of a knowledge society is a vision to overcome the threats of precarization through knowledge. This vision is a driving ethos in a knowledge society. Every citizen contributes to overcoming precarization by acquiring knowledge with which she can play a role in the social process of producing a good life. She cannot and shall not address all singular cases, only those within her professional know-how. Society organizes knowledge professionals so that all cases of precarity get solved. Thus a person can with good conscience, abstract from cases of precarization that are not her business. The knowledge society takes care of them.

Knowledge guides action better than belief, irrational ideas, guesses, hope, tradition, prayers, power, or emotions. Thus Plato coined the love of knowledge, especially knowledge of that which is good. It is the best guidance because it always seeks to improve knowledge. It is best to let knowledge-seeking people with good knowledge do the job rather than believe in authority or hope for emotions and prayers to lead to good work. This leads to the idea of a knowledge society able to eliminate misery and precarization. To Plato, knowledge is significant not only to craftsmanship but especially to governance. Leaders should even possess wisdom.

Being guided by knowledge governance creates a society where the ethos to act based on knowledge of the good life makes everybody—each in their specialty—work to overcome threats of precarization. Specialized knowledge forms professions that limit the range of self-actions one should perform. Other professions should perform actions outside this professional field. The role of governance is to organize this whole so that society produces and distributes the knowledge needed.

Government implements rules to stick to their profession and avoid acting based on empathy when they recognize a problem. Except for special cases, people should not help by doing anything themselves but by calling professionals. Despite this behavior's reasons, it counteracts and alienates some people's desire to help. They feel expelled and precarized, being reduced to not by-standers but by-passers.

The knowledge-oriented ethos makes people be trusted based on their knowledge and understanding. The knowledge society produces knowledge for all social institutions and professions to counter any precarization. Precarization is not inevitable. If there is precarization, it cannot be the (knowledge) society's fault. It may be the fault of nature or of laziness of the precarious, but not of society. The knowledge society is the ideal society.

According to UNESCO, a knowledge society must "build on four pillars: freedom of expression; universal access to information and knowledge; respect for cultural and linguistic diversity; and quality education for all." A knowledge society would counter precarization. However, presently, at the peak of knowledge, these pillars crack. Their success caused them to break and replace knowledge society with confusion, hysteria, and deception.

First, freedom of expression is under attack. It cannot help a precarious person that she has a language and the means to communicate and thus establish social relations and integration if there is no freedom to use it. If she is only allowed to use the language to confirm the narratives used to produce the exclusion and not assert her as a self-active person, then language cannot help her re-integrate.

Second, universal access to information and knowledge is made more available. With a few clicks, a huge horizon of knowledge is available to people. On the other hand, masses of secret knowledge are being collected and protected by governance, and massive spying on people to a degree never seen before plays an increasing role in manipulating and controlling people, organizing covert operations, and deceptive maneuvers by business and governance. Despite the wealth of accessible knowledge, the knowledge that controls people's lives is kept secret. Significant decisions are made based on hidden narratives. While politicians are elected based on their political promises, their politics produce changes contradictory to their promises or not even mentioned. Thus voters do not know what politics they elect.

Third, respect for cultural and linguistic diversity is still far second to dominant Western Eurocentrism. Still, the rule is that Western policies control and command.

Finally, it has become uncertain what quality education means. Knowledge has also been used to produce mass-scale destruction through wars and industrial destruction of the environment because knowledge production has largely been controlled by economic and political power that acted based on short-term interests.

6 Inclusion and Exclusion

Ideally, social organizations—institutions and businesses—complement each other to constitute a network of value systems that covers the activities needed to produce a good life. Their activities should be based on professional knowledge systems driven by values of the good life—self-activity, complementarity, love, creativity, and irreplaceable value.

Major systems are organized in hierarchies to distribute organized power to act. The hierarchies control the level of self-activity of people. When a hierarchy removes power to self-act from a lover level to a higher hierarchical level, it naturally installs a level of precarization, separating lover-level people from controlling their activities. A chain of master–slave dialectic is installed. The network of over-masters is clouded. All other people in the chain are, to some extent, precarious. Their concern for their own position in the hierarchy causes the focus on contributing to the good life to become distant. A one-way, top-down hierarchy installs a master–slave relation that invites using oppressive—thus hostile—control, involves alienation, and excluding precarization to manifest power. Life-hostile ethos may define the climate.

The processes that control a system are communicative patterns. Two types of narratives manage interaction and social control: those driven by an inclusive and those driven by an exclusive ethos.

Top-down structures are based on a one-way command chain. It is upheld and driven by an ethos of exclusion. Either people accept and support the power, or they are excluded. The aim is to suppress self-activity at lower levels to defend the top-down chain.¬¬ To do this, narratives of exclusion are produced. The exclusive ethos eliminates some people, phenomena, or things. This is life-hostile.

Life-friendly language games are, on the other hand, two-way. They are open and receptive both ways. An inclusive ethos drives them. This ethos is social and integrates people, phenomena, or things.

To society, it is important to know who its members are and who is not if it is to take care to protect people and avoid precarization. Inclusive approaches accept all people as part of the society, while exclusive approaches restrict the selection of members by excluding others. For example, workplaces use hiring and firing to include and exclude people.

The underlying logic of inclusion is the conjunction: "A and B and …". They are all counted in. The task is not to enumerate all. It is to integrate them, i.e., establish social relations of complementary activities through which everybody contributes. Inclusion is complicated because it involves integrating the self-activity of the hitherto not integrated.

This presupposes creativity and the development of new ideas. Thus it may be an opportunity for innovation and development.

The underlying logic of exclusion is the exclusive disjunction: "Either A or B or … ". Some are counted in, and some are counted out. The process of exclusion defends a status quo and may cause stagnation.

Society must regulate the system of practices from an inclusive perspective to integrate all people. If society does not fulfill this task, some people are excluded and become precarized. The precarious people are standing outside society although still a living part of it. Exclusion is not life-friendly.

Some modes are in-between inclusion and exclusion. Logically, the inclusive disjunction might capture this third possibility: "Either A or B or C or … maybe all of them." However, in many situations, it is unclear whether people are included or excluded in many situations. Thus there are three types of social status: to be in, out, and questionable. To be questionable is also precarizing. It reflects precarization by alienation. Thus there are two forms of precarization: the questionable and alienated and the excluded.

6.1 Inclusive Ethos

Society uses inclusion narratives to legitimize inclusive policies. Inclusion is based on a life-friendly ethos aiming at a good life. It involves being part of the social community or simply being social. Inclusion is based on positive values that provide a reason for the inclusion. Traditionally, these values include equality, human rights, tolerance, and non-discrimination. However, although these values are politically significant, they are associated with a passive perception of life and a dualist mind–body perspective. They may support a friendly ethos, but they miss life-friendliness. They overlook that life is being active! And especially life's self-active character! Which therefore is what the values should protect and improve. Thus they do not express an understanding of life thus, neither of the good life. Guiding the development of notions of the good life are observable value signals such as thriving, self-activity, creativity, complementarity in behavior, being inspired by the diversity and creativity of others, helpfulness, and liking life.

The activity of inclusion is integrating. People are equal but different. Thus inclusion must enable them to use their differences to supplement each other and thus create complementary structures of activities. This creates joy to contribute to the performance. In an inclusive narrative, people are not all the same type, but all living beings a in love of life. Integrating the different creates life and dynamics. By being equal but different, each person develops a unique identity representing an irreplaceable value. And the inclusive ethos simultaneously establishes the narrative that people and society can be trusted to help when in need. There is a typical positive value load: Human beings are good loving beings. The inclusive ethos is an ethic of benevolence and love. It aims at fairness and avoids bias. It is about life-friendliness.

Some believe that fear and pressure are necessary to make people creative, whereas 'good inclusion' makes them lazy and un-innovative: 'Aggressive motivation helps to make things move.' These ideas may be associated with Darwinian or market economic survival ideas by 'innovation' in a harsh and competitive environment. However, even the development of a species starts with an innovation (mutation) in an individual and spreads to the species from there if the environment prefers it. Nature's development is slow compared to human development, which is based on innovative ideas. Humans are especially innovative; they thrive by producing ideas and trying new things. The more creative people that cooperate, the greater the innovative results can be if they work in an inclusive atmosphere that nourishes and develops ideas in an environment that has developed integrative skills and endeavors. A plurality of ideas is brought to work in the innovative, integrative processes that change the world. That is how human beings developed life form after life form.

Replacing integration with exclusion stops this innovative, creative process. The one-eyed top-down control only allows a few ideas. It is unable and unwilling to integrate a plurality of ideas and make the many bright people synchronize their creative, intelligent ideas to create a performance at a higher level.

6.2 Exclusive Ethos

While the inclusive ethos manifests flexibility and openness for integrating many possible solutions, the exclusive ethos claims that there is one solution. It is the necessary thing to do. The rest, i.e., the different, must be excluded. This legitimates the dictatorial use of force and intolerance. Intolerance against the deviant replaces the inclusive appreciation of difference. Since people may not deviate, they are all the same, and there is no creative drive. Changes are quantitative more or less of the same; there is no qualitative conceptual development. The system is inflexible and sluggish. Deviant reflection is considered a threat and, therefore, oppressed. People that advocate alternatives are considered enemies to be combatted and precarized.

Guided by this ethos, exclusion narratives are used to establish reasons to exclude deviant people from the community. These are discriminatory narratives in which the discriminating gatekeeper—leader or media—is positioned as good and right while the victim is bad. These narratives create a bias against a victim. They are narratives of 'we/the form 'I (we) are good, she/the other is bad.' The other is inferior, bad, evil, untrustworthy, and dangerous; they are lazy, enemies, criminals, oppressors, thieves, and murderers and must be targeted for destruction. It is a story of hate and aggression. It undermines social relations and fosters destruction, suffering, and even death. The reason for defining the other as evil is to legitimize actions to alienate and exclude her.

The unethical nature of such a narrative is obvious. It has no merit. It is based on lies and deception. And it aims at destruction and suffering. This is a classic strategy against a desired enemy. It is often used by a social power that intends to perform acts much more terrible than anything the victim has done. Thus it turns out that the exclusive ethos and the narratives it uses are the real culprits of evil. Users of exclusion narratives to victimize others make themselves unethical and life-hostile. They exemplify a special unethical ethics, namely the ethics that condemns the other for doing something bad to legitimize doing something bad or even worse oneself.

The discriminatory ethos installs a paranoiac mindset that undermines cognition and logic. Since it has a biased purpose, everything about the narrator, the 'I' or 'we' is a priori good. And everything that about 'the victim is a priori bad. It is good when we do it because it is us, the good ones. It is bad when the other does it because she is the bad one. This 'reasoning' uses the conclusion to prove the premises. The conclusion is an axiom. Thus it is a paranoiac. This is the logic this ethos installs with its narratives. It does not matter if the same is said about both sides. This feature makes it paranoiac. Its logic excludes any objectivity. The evidence does not determine whether something is good or not, as in common healthy cognition. It does not matter what it is. If we do it, it is good; if the victim does it, then it is bad. This dissolves reason, replacing it with hysteria against the victim.

Paranoiac narratives are constructed through the selection of a target that then continuously is smeared so that people start believing that the victim is bad, although the smearing is a narrative without any merit. It then produces hysteria by nourishing emotions again without any real reason. This disrupts the mindset that nourishes a knowledge society, replacing it with hysteria. Such communicative techniques are used by leaders and media against singular persons, groups, countries, and cultures. It creates a mindset of hate and destruction by making people believe that others are barbaric, dangerous and that they must be destroyed. Thus the self-good ones are the destroyers.

The exclusion narrative undermines the nature of society in general. It undermines the trustworthiness of communication in general. In an exclusive mindset, the good people must prevent the bad from obtaining knowledge and information about actual conditions because that would make them strong. Thus communication with the bad people or those the bad can observe must be misleading but still sound trustworthy. With such ethos, no relevant public communication can be trustworthy.

Further, nobody can feel safe in this environment whether she receives trustworthy information. Without knowing it, she may be considered an enemy and, therefore, a person, that must be lied to. Leaders who use their presumably loyal people in a conflict against an enemy may nevertheless worry that some of them are enemies. Being dictatorial, leaders suspect their subordinates to be opponents, therefore untrustworthy and possibly dangerous. The intricateness of the precarization dynamics of an exclusive ethos shows that reason and good life have a difficult time in such environments. Communication, the heart of the social, may be almost indistinguishable from deceptive gaming.

6.3 The Urgency Argument

The argument that one must act now because it is urgent and there is no time for reflection and analysis is characteristic of the exclusion ethos. The matter is portrayed as catastrophic if one acts slowly. The point of the argument is to override the reflection process that might find more reasonable conclusions than the life-hostile course of exclusion and destruction. The use of this argument without even documenting that it is that urgent illustrates the violent character of this ethos. It aims at avoiding solutions that are life-friendly and activates qualified actors that can produce smart creative solutions without aggression by exclusion.

A reflective both-and-mindset of inclusive ethos does take more time than the fight-or-fly responses of the reptile brain. The improvement of the reaction obtained by investing time to reflect and analyze normally improves the outcome significantly. And the claim that time is urgent is seldom documented when made by an exclusion ethos. It plays to the hands of hysteria, not reason. Reason considers all the relevant aspects. It would be urgent if reason was used to call for urgent reaction. Even then, using moments reflecting on the best decision would be better than listening to emotional hysteria. Suppose a call for an urgent reaction is not based on credible reason. In that case, an exclusive mindset plays games to obtain a strategic or tactical advantage over a chosen victim.

However, the urgency argument is engraved in the modern economy, where everything may seem urgent. 'The fastest are the winners in the competition,' is the imagined rule. To increase productivity and turnover, governance pushes people to hurry and avoid time for reflection. Modern life is infected by this rush, being busy to reach something—the end of the tunnel.

The last century saw many parliamentary regimes being toppled by fascist groups because they were too slow and unable to cope with society's problems. Fascist systems replaced their inclusive reflection with aggression and exclusion based on one idea, that of the leader. Normally, taking time to produce a well-reflected reaction solves the problem faster and better than hysterical 'spontaneous' reactions, which are likely to cause extra problems.

The narrative leading to the Second Iraq War is an example of the urgency argument. According to the narrative, Iraq threatened the (western) world by developing weapons of mass destruction. The weapons were about to be ready. Thus a preemptive strike to prevent the disaster was urgent. This narrative was absurd. The idea that Iraq should pose a threat to the world had no merit whatsoever. It was a total fabrication. Nevertheless, the aggressors managed to create the desired hysteria through lying narratives which enabled a full-scale attack on Iraq by a group of war-hungry countries, launching immense suffering due to the destruction of the country and the death of possibly 500.000 Iraqis. If reason and a life-friendly and inclusive ethos had driven these countries, then there would have been no war, destruction, or mass death. The lies of the exclusive narrative would have been revealed. Instead, cooperation would have developed productive relations to benefit all.

There is no reason to assume that the attacking countries' population is especially war-hungry. Their war hysteria was created by massive propaganda. A comprehensive system of deception was activated to fool people, precarizing the whole population and overruling the voices of knowledge and reason, especially that of UN investigator C. Bildt. Many social leaders that ought to have raised the alarm over the aggressive nonsense were also fooled and thus precarized, unable to function properly as democratic leaders. Other political leaders were part of the deceptive plot for whatever reason.—This case is one of many cases where the media have created a hysteric paranoiac of deception by selectively targeting a leader leading to an attack and destruction of the country. It illustrates that one of the worst things for a country is precarized leaders. It is worst for the victim but also bad for the aggressive country whose population lives in a world of fiction, that they are the good ones although they destroy and kill.

The power of the exclusive ethos is concerning. It is concerning that human populations so readily accept leaders with strong life-hostile exclusive ethos. The great peace broke out in about 1990 and should have put the war drums to rest forever. Instead, the war drums were silenced but had maintained their power structure intact in the form of NATO, a war machine that had lost its purpose and needed a new one. Since the end of the 1990th, media and governance have used the ethos of exclusion to attack a list of countries, first by media hysteria that painted the victim as a devil to fear and then by warfare. The dark ethos is in full operation and in full swing to create future wars. The propagation of hate replaces diplomacy for peace, understanding, and cooperation. The period of peace is transformed into a period of hate and wars, one after the other. There are many layers of action and actors, known and secret, in this process. The media do not uncover this. Instead, they are part of it and deceive and create mass hysteria to avoid scholarly analysis. When people are led by deceptive narratives—whether by religion or mass media—their self-activity is manipulated. They are precarized by alienation. Their illusion that they live in a knowledge society makes them believe and thus prisoners of the deception.

It is not easy to understand the motives behind the ethics of destruction. What are the motives for producing suffering and death? It could be greed. But why could greedy people not make money by doing something good? They must have a desire to produce terror and destruction. What other motive is there? If there are good and decent reasons, why have they been kept so secret? The media tell the story: 'We, the good and innocent people, are threatened by the evil X. We must hurry to destroy this threat before it becomes real. This is an act of legitimate self-defense.' The real destruction and suffering of the life of people caused by this act are not considered relevant.

The covid-19 event also displayed an urgency-motivated hysteria driven by the media to legitimate aggressive policies that precarized the whole population with lockdown, masks, social distancing, and almost forced vaccination. This time, ' big pharma' functioned as an underlying motivator. But, again, the motive of greed is obvious.

In the aftermath of the pandemic, a lot of criticism has emerged amongst others: The credibility of the hysterical narration, the exaggeration of the precarizing precautions due to their negative effects, the excessive vaccinations now blamed as possible causes for increased mortality levels after the pandemic; lies and secrecy concerning the effects of the vaccine; and the secrecy of the deals between the industry and the politicians. The hysteria enabled governance to sideline reason in their preventive measures and oppress professional criticism. The analysis of and reactions to the event are still ongoing.

Considering the basis of a knowledge society, it may be wise to recall the advice from R. Descartes, one of the founders of the Enlightenment: "It is prudent never to trust those who have deceived us, even if only once." The reality of an enormous mass deception created by mass media is so clear and well-documented in the case of the second Iraq war that it is prudent never to trust them. They are destructive of the knowledge society.

7 The Social Compact

7.1 Views from Nowhere

Based on T. Nagel's philosophy, mass media journalism has been criticized for presenting their reporting as representing the objective truth and, therefore, as credible and not biased. The criticism would agree with Myrdal that the reporting is subjective and thus biased, which should be made obvious.

Nagel opens an alternative to the subjectivity perspective by introducing the view from nowhere. He contrasts passive and active points of view on the relationship with the world. A subjective perspective reflects a specific, active, and biased point of view. A scientific point of view is, however, an objective point of view and, therefore, a view from nowhere and, consequently, a passive and unbiased view.—This is quite different from my reaction to Myrdal's position above. My reaction is that the opposite of bias is not objectivity but being encompassing. All affected subjects must be included and be allowed to express their views.

The criticism of journalism, thus, is that they pretend to write from nowhere and, therefore, objectively and thus unbiased. It is significant—and, however, a problem to the critique—that objectivity and a view from nowhere seem to be different things confused by the use of Nagel's analysis. The criticism is correct that influential journalism applies a view from nowhere, especially concerning international affairs, but this does not make them objective. Objectivity on worldly matters is bound to specific points of view in time and space. (There is no absolute space and time.) That which has no specific point of view and thus is a view from nowhere is the abstract.

In the Second Iraq War, excited people could follow the bombs on their TV, targeting and exploding the bunkers where Iraqi people were hiding, almost like a war movie in a cinema only this was no movie. A horrible mass killing was taking place by these bombs. The later wars have not repeated this perverse show. The ethos of the knowledge society wanted specific evidence, and the show offered just that. However, it also became clear after the war that the whole war propaganda was a scam, built on lies, without any merit. While the bombs presumably were specific and true, the lies about mass destruction and the threats to the world Iraq posed were not. Both operated within the ethos of a knowledge society: respect for evidence that trances claims to the specific in time and space. The terrible thing is that this is objectivity and not some subjective imagination as a movie. It is, however, biased only showing the side of the heroes sending the marvelous bombs defending the West, not of the victims being bombed. It is not a view from nowhere but from US fighter jets and the American war machine.

Journalistic reports since that amazing show have been much less specific. It is as if they have discovered that a view from nowhere is a safer point of view. The Iraq project was, after all, revealed as based on pure swindling. Narratives that are views from nowhere are much more difficult to reveal. There are no specifications that may be used to produce evidence. Make political narratives like fairy tales. They cannot be disproven. They need some names, the victims, but the media construct stories about their intentions instead of evidence about what they intend and do. Nobody listens to them. Thus nobody can disprove this. One may still put in some spy photos, although that may be risky. It may remind some people on C. Powel with photos of Iraq's facilities for weapons of mass destruction at the UN.

The view from nowhere is more than just scientific. It is also a view of fiction used to gaslight people. And a view of fiction that pretends to be real. From a position of nowhere, one cannot report anything about the world because one cannot observe anything. Thus, by reporting from a view of nowhere, they only need to hide that there are very few real specificities beyond names they defame or prize. This strategy is used by the media and many in society—in personal relations, governance, and leadership. The cognitive spirit of the knowledge society has been replaced by a spirit of gaming where winners activate emotional reactions.

The alternative to subjective bias is versatile, comprehensive, multi-subjective reporting that includes the perspectives of all those affected. It is not a view from nowhere but a view from 'many-where.' To ensure fairness in reporting the views of those affected, they must be allowed to present their opinion on how they are reported. If they are not allowed to do that. Their critique of a report of their view may be misleading. Only by presenting such disagreements openly can people make an informed judgment. Their reaction is precarious if they are prevented from making an informed judgment, then their reaction is precarious.

7.2 The Abstract-Specific Gap

An important technique of deceptive communication in the present precarizing society is avoiding linking the narrative to the specifics, i.e., letting the narrative appear as a real story. In reality, it is fiction made from nowhere. There is rarely never any real evidence. There is a gap between the specific and the abstract. If this gap is bridged, there can be evidence and the narrative real. To be bridged, the narrative must be about specifics to which it can be traced. A good epistemic tradition for such tracing characterizes a knowledge society, that loves knowledge and avoids policies made on pure emotions. Without secure links bridging the abstract-specific gap, there is no knowledge. Knowledge enables people to avoid precarious conditions. The work of science created a knowledge society that replaced arbitrary commands of leaders that had everybody at their mercy with inclusive, knowledgeable practices. Based on scientific attitudes, abstract narratives were linked to the specifics of practice by verified links. The abstract narratives were taken out of nowhere and put to work in specific conditions through these links.

Concepts have abstract meanings (also called their content or intension). This meaning is nowhere. They may also have a scope of specific things in the world that they apply to (also called their reference or extension). The specifics may exist or be fictive. Whether or not a concept has a scope is decided by observation. There is however no a priori link between abstract meaning and the specific observable phenomena. Such links cannot be made by observation, because one cannot make observations without them. Thus there is a gap between the abstract and the specifics of the world. The abstract world may be analyzed by logic and reasoning. The empirical world is studied by observational data. The gap must be bridged to analyze and organize.

The solution is that people that communicate constantly produce speech acts that create links to bridge these gaps wherever it is needed. These speech acts are social agreements. These acts are compacts. Their criteria, whether a compact is good, is pragmatic, whether it serves its purpose. The gaslighting strategies, that penetrate much of modern communication avoid committing to any bridges while luring people to believe that certain obvious bridges were made.

The abstract meaning of concepts are stated in lexica and textbooks. The late Wittgenstein considered the meaning in use—not the abstract lexical meaning—to be the real meaning. The abstract meaning is a proto-meaning, vague model that helps people to create the specific meaning of actual usage where the concepts are related to specific phenomena. Abstract concepts are used to make many different specific concepts. Both abstract and specific concepts develop and change over time. There are many techniques to specify the abstract concepts to make them usable. There are for instance, pronouns used in ostensive definitions, specifying definitions, and implicit definitions in body language used to attach the abstract concept to specific observations. Normally it is presumed that people, through their education, know established compacts so that one does not need to explain the meaning every time a concept is used.—Since most concepts have several interpretations this is a way to avoid committing to one compact i.e., to speak from nowhere. It is doing as if one knows, although nobody knows what is meant because nothing is being meant.

7.3 The Social Compact

Life and all its activities are specific. Therefore the abstract-specific gap must be bridged for communication to have practical meaning. If this gap cannot be crossed then social reality disappears. With no communication to organize inter-activities, there is no social world. This is, therefore, the golden bridge, the bridge of hope. It is the bridge into the social world.

To create the bridge, people specify their concepts to fit specific uses. It is an act of specification, a speech act, that bridges the gap. The language users create the speech act and bridge the gap. It is not created in the language defined in abstract terms a priori before its use. Users create it while they use it. This speech act creates a compact agreement between the speakers to share this specified meaning of the abstract concept. This is their meaning in use. Before the specification, the abstract concept was to them like an unfinished prototype.

The compact is a social compact. It not only finishes the meaning of the conceptual prototype, making it fit for use, but it also creates a social relation between the 'shareholders' of the compact. They share a common understanding and trust. People do not have a social relationship before agreeing on the specific meaning of the abstract. This compact is a 'golden bridge'. It integrates people and enables them to cooperate. It is the basic form of inclusion. Sharing a compact is inclusion.

People that are excluded from sharing the compact are being precarized. They are isolated from communication and will consequently lose touch with the net of compacts that develop in the community. Their way out of the community is a way to nowhere, a place where words only have abstract meaning.

The ability to make a compact is always present when people meet. There are proto-social situations. R. Harré presented the following image of the social, which may illustrate the transition from the proto-social to the social via creating shared compacts: two strangers meet on a narrow path on a steep mountainside. One rushes down, the other up. They cannot pass without careful interaction. This is a proto-social relation. They do not push each other aside as if they were rolling stones. They first establish a social relationship by slowing down and looking at each other as they approach, creating mutual awareness of the other and the situation. Then they stop, greet each other friendly, and make a little small talk to see if they can communicate, mutually understand, and trust each other. What happens then depends on how this proto-social activity plays out. To pass, they must find a way to trust each other. When trust has been created, a social relationship is established. Now they can cooperate and start planning how precisely to interact to pass safely. All the initial steps are compacts to ensure they dared cooperate to pass.

Communication in practice is based on sharing compacts in all the aspects where a specification is needed to bridge the abstract-specific gaps to cooperate. Making shared compacts is the most widespread speech act in effective communication. It is basic in the learning of language.

The exclusive ethos needs strategies to confuse the other, the enemies, or the victims. Communication that is open or directed to them is likely to use deceptive strategies. It is a problem that this information spreads to their people too thus their people unknowingly become their enemies. Society gets flooded with exclusion narratives, hidden information, and leaked hidden information. Information on all people accumulates secretly to manipulate the population.

7.4 Conceptual Illusions

There are different ways to bridge the abstract and the specific. First, there is a way of honest clarification. For example, the concept 'red'.' By pointing out a paradigm of red, one somewhat specifies the concept. When a person points at a pink color and asks: Is this also red, a new compact is made by the denial. In other circumstances, the pink color may be included. This is about clarifying the concept in practice because it attempts to find a color that matches the abstract imagination of red. Alternatively, suppose the person asking is considered an enemy; then someone might produce a misleading answer, show her a green color, and call it red. This is a deceptive compact. A person may come into many troubles through mistaking red and green.

Deceptive compacts create a mismatch between abstract content and the phenomena referred to. They produce conceptual illusions. As above, conceptual illusions may serve to embellish, slander, or simply mislead. Illusions of embellishments seem to be involved in concepts like 'democracy.' While the practice is that people in many so-called democratic countries have little to say (this is the reality of the reference), the abstract content of the concept says that the people rule the country. The concept of leadership is also often used to produce illusion. The abstract meaning of 'leader' is leading people, helping them solve problems and find good solutions. In practice, many leaders do nothing in that direction but give orders, manipulate, and control. The relation between the abstract meaning and the specific reference in practice is often deceptive. It indicates a culture that distances itself from scholarly criteria characteristic of a knowledge society. A communication culture characterized by hysteria and ethics of exclusion makes it impossible for people to trust the decision processes. The whole society is in a precarious situation. Focus on life friendliness, honest clarification, inclusion, and abstaining from ethics of exclusion is the way out of precarization. It creates the social and enables bonding, thus creating a unique value and good life.

8 The Proto-Social and Final Precarization

The proto-social is that which we have a priori to the social. It is its genesis. Of course, our proto-social condition is our love of life. And life friendliness is, therefore, the way to a good social life, and loss of life friendliness is loss of the social and thus precarization. In practice, we are guided by imaginations that give us a feeling of meaning. The philosophy of meaning should guide us to life-friendliness and the good life.

Basic to life is securing the relation to its environment. Empiricist epistemologies try to explain meaning as the meaning of abstract terms by linking sense observation, which is specific, with the abstract. Abstract concepts that are not based on observation are metaphysical misnomers. Specifically, the verification theory of the meaning of logical positivism assumed that the meaning of words is a function of observable sense data. This notion has been implemented in operational definitions of concepts in questionnaires as outlined in books on methodology. However, the verification theory of meaning failed. It could find no values. It reduced them to subjective bias. To this, we reply that the goodness of life is observable—the thriving, the lively self-activity, the happy spirit, etc. Further. It was impossible to define abstract concepts in sense data terms. We explained this by analyzing the relationship between abstract and specific meaning. Abstract terms have an abstract proto meaning. They, therefore, need additional speech acts to give them a specific meaning as the basis for their use in practice. This is our use theory of meaning. The guideline for the specification is pragmatic, based on action, and not empiricist. The meaning is the use. The final meaning of a concept in use is not given with a lexical definition because it is abstract. The emphasis on contingency and contextual conditions in many studies underscores this condition.

Thus we use the theory of meaning-is-use by the late Wittgenstein to understand the specific meaning that functions in practice. It presupposes, however, abstract proto-meaning that is used to create the specifying compact. This theory shifts the understanding of meaning from the lexical and abstract meaning to the specific meaning in use, which fits the understanding of life as an activity. Moreover, it is pragmatic and dynamic. It is my interpretation of Wittgenstein's theory that meaning-is-use, that he here specifies that the meaning is about something specific. Because use, action, and life are specific- not abstract.

Although the theory of meaning-as-use distances meaning from abstract lexical meaning. However, abstract meaning plays an important role in the formation of specifying compacts. The abstract meaning is a view from nowhere. On the one hand, it is like a cloud of possible compacts. On the other hand, it is something logical that binds the concepts in a constitutive network that enables theoretical reflection. In theoretical reflection, abstract meaning is specified by other abstract terms. The world of abstract concepts is an overwhelming interconnected network of concepts whose interconnections can be interpreted and specified in many ways. That which connects it to the world is the cloud of possible compacts that are attached to the concepts. Practice and reflection interact to create the needed operative compacts.

Human mind lives with these interwoven clouds and logics where any concepts can produce ideas that illuminate parts of the world like new lenses and enjoy new sides of the world and produce new forms of interactivities around special shared lenses. Each person has a cosmos of concepts and clouds. This cosmos is a proto-social world. Any imagination is there—every face, living being, art, fantasy memory, every idea, wild and weird, simple and beautiful. It is a fascinating world, enlightened by happiness. And everybody uses sides of it in practice and in inter-play and -joy. And everybody develops and explores sides of it, and in her mind, she makes discoveries and enlarges it. She may share her discoveries with others. And the social ethos of inclusion loves these contributions.—Unless people on their way are precarized and locked in the outside social position, having dropped the inclusive ethos, they welcome these contributions if they can understand just some of it. Precarization is not final and fatal before there is no more road from the proto-social exploration to the social. That is if everybody on her road has closed their mind and turned their back on life.—Again, there is an 'unless': unless she has given up on her inner self, the source of her power, contribution, and joy. This is the final precarization.

Conclusion: We can transform the distinction between competence and performance to define the condition of social versus precarization. The ability to co-construct compacts and cope with working compacts of social networks is the competence with which precarization is avoided. The performance to integrate with the social network is the use of operating compacts in the language games of the social network. Participation in language games without coping with the operating compacts creates fake communication and precarization.

Further Reading

Burnham, G., Lafta, R., Doocy, S., & Roberts, L. (2006). Mortality after the 2003 invasion of Iraq: a cross-sectional cluster sample survey *Internet ArchiveWayBackMachine*. https://web.archive.org/web/20150907130701/ http://brusselstribunal.org/pdf/lancet111006.pdf. Retrieved November 2006.

Chomsky, N. (1965). *Aspects of the theory of syntax*. MIT Press.

Descartes, R. (1641). *Meditations of first Philosophy. Meditation I. Latin original title*: Meditationes de prima philosophia.

Drucker, P. F. (1969). *Coined the concept "knowledge society" in The age of discontinuity: Guidelines to our changing society*. Harper & Row.

Guardian Datablok. (2023). *Wikileaks Iraq: data journalism maps every death*. https://www.theguardian.com/news/datablog/2010/oct/23/wikileaks-iraq-data-journalism#data

Hegel, A. (2018). *Phenomenology of the spirit*. Cambridge University Press.

Hume, D. (1739). *A treatise on human nature*. John Noon.
Maras, S. (2013). "The view from nowhere". Objectivity in journalism. In *Key concepts in journalism* (pp. 77–81). Polity Press.
Moore: Principia Ethica. (1903). Cambridge University Press.
Myrdal, G. (1969). *Objectivity in social research*. Random House Trade Paperbacks.
Nagel, T. (1989). *View from nowhere*. Oxford University Press.
Nørreklit, L. (2020). A pragmatic constructivist perspective on language games. *Proceedings of Pragmatic Constructivism, 10*(1), 11–28. https://doi.org/10.7146/propracon.v10i1.119252
Nørreklit, L. (2021). The language game of goodness. *Journal of Pragmatic Constructivism, 11*, 1. https://doi.org/10.7146/jopracon.v11i1.127249
Paulsen, M., & Nørreklit, L. (Working paper). *Life-friendliness and Philopathy: Towards life-friendly language games.*
Plato (1968/360 B.C). *The Republic. See e.g. Bloom, Allan. The Republic of Plato*. Basic Books.
Rosen, J. (November 10, 2010). The view from nowhere: questions and answers. *pressthink.org*. Retrieved October10, 2017.
de Saussure, F. (1960). *Course in general linguistics*. Peter Owen.
UNESCO. (2023). https://en.unesco.org/70years/knowledge_societies_way_forward_better_world
Wittgenstein, L. (1922). *Tractatus Logico-Philosophicus*. Kegan Paul.
Wittgenstein, L. (1956). *Philosophical investigations*. Basil Blackwell.

GPSR Compliance
The European Union's (EU) General Product Safety Regulation (GPSR) is a set of rules that requires consumer products to be safe and our obligations to ensure this.

If you have any concerns about our products, you can contact us on

ProductSafety@springernature.com

In case Publisher is established outside the EU, the EU authorized representative is:

Springer Nature Customer Service Center GmbH
Europaplatz 3
69115 Heidelberg, Germany

www.ingramcontent.com/pod-product-compliance
Ingram Content Group UK Ltd.
Pitfield, Milton Keynes, MK11 3LW, UK
UKHW040225290926
15471UKWH00001B/4
9783658430405